ASK SUZE®

. . . ABOUT PLANNING FOR

YOUR FUTURE

Riverhead Books
a member of
Penguin Group (USA) Inc.
New York
2007

ASK SUZE®

◆

...ABOUT PLANNING FOR YOUR FUTURE

SUZE ORMAN

This publication is designed to provide accurate and authoritative information in regard to the subject matter covered. It is published with
the understanding that the publisher and author are not engaged in
rendering legal, accounting, or other professional services. If legal advice or other professional advice, including financial, is required, the
services of a competent professional person should be sought.

While the author has made every effort to provide accurate telephone
numbers and Internet addresses at the time of publication, neither the
publisher nor the author assumes any responsibility for errors, or for
changes that occur after publication.

Ask Suze® is a federally registered mark owned by Suze Orman.

People First, Then Money, Then Things™ is a trademark owned by
Suze Orman.

Certified Financial Planner® is a federally registered mark owned by
the Certified Financial Planner Board of Standards, Inc.

The term Realtor® is a collective membership mark owned by the National Association of Realtors® and refers to a real estate agent who is a
member thereof.

RIVERHEAD BOOKS
a member of
Penguin Group (USA) Inc.
375 Hudson Street
New York, NY 10014

ISBN 978-1-59448-968-6

Printed in the United States of America
1   3   5   7   9   10   8   6   4   2

Book design by Deborah Kerner and Claire Vaccaro

ASK
SUZE®

. . . ABOUT PLANNING FOR
YOUR FUTURE

PUTTING YOUR MONEY TO WORK

As Americans live longer, we will spend an increasing number of years living on our retirement incomes. We know that we can't count primarily on Social Security to provide this income and that, if we wish to maintain a comfortable standard of living during a long retirement, many of us will have to rely primarily on our retirement savings.

This chapter is intended to guide you to a safe and comfortable retirement. The questions and answers will help you to plan well for the years ahead. They include crucial information about funding and withdrawing funds from 401(k)s, IRAs, stock option plans, and many of the other retirement programs that may be available to you.

The tax advantages of today's retirement plans allow your savings to grow far more quickly and effectively than ordinary, taxed savings vehicles can. Please invest in as many of them as you are eligible for. If you have doubts about the best investment choices for your retirement plan, seek guidance from a good professional adviser who can help you construct a sensible financial profile (you'll find some tips on hiring a professional in *Ask Suze . . . About Stocks and Bonds*). But whether you're investing with the help of an adviser or alone, don't forget that it's your money that's at stake. Watch your investments carefully. It's a matter of securing your dreams.

For more information about investing techniques, please see *Ask Suze . . . About Stocks and Bonds* and *Ask Suze . . . About Mutual Funds and Annuities*.

RETIREMENT PLANS

How many different kinds of retirement plans are available?

The answer depends on whether you are an employee or are self-employed. Below is a list of the most popular retirement plans. Most are for use by employees of companies; the plans with an asterisk are typically limited to those with self-employment income. Entries marked with a Q are qualified plans, which means that employers can receive a tax break for their contributions to these plans.

Defined-Benefit Plan—Q
Target-Benefit Plan—Q
Defined-Contribution Plan—Q
Profit-Sharing Plan—Q
Money-Purchase Pension Plan—Q
Stock Bonus Plan—Q
457 Plan
401(k)—Q
Roth (401)—Q
403(b)
TSA
Traditional IRA

Roth IRA
Converted Roth IRA
Rollover IRA
*SIMPLE IRA
*SEP-IRA
*Keogh Plan—Q

What is a qualified retirement plan?

A qualified retirement plan is what large companies usually offer to their employees. As defined by section 401 of the U.S. Tax Code, qualified plans were created as a tax incentive for employers to contribute to employee retirement plans. Every year, your employer is allowed to deduct from company taxes certain contributions it makes to the plan on your behalf.

What are the benefits of qualified retirement plans?

The advantage to you as an employee is that your contributions in a qualified plan are made with pretax dollars from your paycheck. This means that you are not only investing your money for the future, but you are also using a percentage of money that otherwise would have gone to Uncle Sam. Better still, your pretax dollars grow tax-deferred—that is, you don't have to pay any income taxes on your contributions or your investment gains until funds are withdrawn from the plan at retirement. This is also true of certain other retirement-savings vehicles, such as a traditional IRA.

Another advantage is that many employers match part or all of employee contributions. Qualified plans also qualify for special taxation rules such as ten-year averaging and capital-gains tax.

But the most comforting feature of a qualified plan is that it is protected against claims by your employer's creditors. Your money is held in trust for you and should be relatively safe.

Is a qualified retirement plan tied to my employer? What if I change jobs?

Under most circumstances, you can take a qualified retirement plan with you, so to speak, when you change employers. By transferring your retirement account to another retirement vehicle, even one held at a private bank or brokerage company (this is known as an IRA rollover), you can avoid tax consequences. In some cases you may be able to transfer your old retirement plan directly to your new employer's plan.

If my company has a qualified retirement plan, who can participate?

A qualified plan cannot discriminate; all eligible employees can participate. (Some companies may have a waiting period before new employees can participate in their retirement plan.)

Is there such a thing as a nonqualified plan? What is it?

A nonqualified plan does not meet certain IRS or Employee Retirement Income Security Act (ERISA) requirements, so, among other things, it can be used to disproportionately reward employees at higher income levels in a company. (This is something that, by law, qualified plans can't do.) Employees who participate in nonqualified plans have a lot more flexibility and freedom in organizing their investments while still participating in tax-deferred growth. There are few vesting requirements, if any, in a nonqualified plan—in other words, contributions basically belong to the employee as soon as they are made. But there *are* restrictions. Participants in a nonqualified plan may not be able to transfer their money into another retirement account. If they leave the company where their plan is managed, or if they retire, they may have to withdraw all the money in the plan as a lump-sum payment and pay ordinary income tax on it. Also, the assets of the employees are not held in trust, so they are not protected against the claims of the employer's creditors.

Few of the plans covered in this book (except for the 457 plan) are nonqualified plans.

Are most retirement plans governed by the same rules in regard to how long money has to stay in the plan and what happens when it is withdrawn?
Yes. Almost all retirement plans, except Roth IRAs and 457 plans, are governed by very similar withdrawal and taxation rules. In most cases you cannot take money out of your retirement plans prior to the age of 59½. If you do make a withdrawal before you turn 59½, the money you take will be taxed as ordinary income and you will have to pay a 10 percent early-withdrawal penalty to the IRS, as well as a possible state penalty and taxes on that level. You also _must_ start taking money out by April 1 of the year after you turn 70½. At this age, there is a minimum you must withdraw from your retirement account, a figure based on a formula devised by the plan. If you fail to withdraw the minimum, the IRS will assess a 50 percent penalty on that amount. Of course, after the age of 59½, you can take out any amount of money you want—there is no maximum. Just remember that whatever you take out will be taxed as ordinary income.

THE HOWS AND WHYS OF RETIREMENT PLANNING

I know that planning for retirement is important, but I'm always trying to catch up with my bills. When do I really have to start?

I don't even need to know how old you are to answer this question: The time is *right now*. Here's why: Time is the most important factor in the growth of your money. The more time your money is given to grow, the more money you will have when you retire, and the earliest money you contribute grows the most. Planning and investing for your future are signs of self-respect. Start now.

My goal is to save and invest $100 a month for my retirement, but first I want to make a couple of substantial purchases. I'm only 25 years old. How much difference will a few years make?

A few years will make a big, big difference! Let's say you decide to start putting $100 a month in a good no-load mutual fund now, at age 25. Over the years, the fund does very well, averaging a 12 percent return per year. How much will you have when you turn 65? Almost $1,000,000. Now, let's examine what will happen if you make those large purchases instead. Say you wait ten years to start investing $100 a month. You may think, no big deal, in ten years I'll be only 35, and how much difference can $1,200 a year, or $12,000 over ten years, really make? It's going to cost you big-time: about $700,000. That's right—if you wait until you are 35 to start investing that $100 a month, you will have only $300,000 at age 65. Wait until you are 45 to start, and you will have only $97,000. If you think time doesn't matter, you are wrong!

Why does time have such a dramatic effect on the growth of money?

The answer involves one of the all-time winning financial concepts: compound returns, sometimes known as compound interest. Compounding creates advantages beyond the obvious benefits of saving and accumulating money. The longer you continue to save, of course, the more you will amass in your retirement account(s). But it's also true that the longer your money is invested, the more money your original contributions can earn—all by themselves—for you.

Here's how it works: Let's say you invest $6,000 a year in your 401(k) account, which earns an average annual return of 8 percent. Let's say you do this for 20 years. The first year, your money will earn $480 in interest, or increased equity value. The next year, as you make your second $6,000 contribution, the account will automatically be returning 8 percent not only on your contributions but also on the first year's $480 gains. The gains on $12,480 (your two original $6,000 contributions, plus the $480 return) are about $998. If you continue to contribute $6,000 every year, and the account continues to earn an 8 percent average annual return, within a decade the annual gain your account earns will be greater than your annual $6,000 contribution. Eventually, the annual gain will be many times greater than your annual contribution to your account.

To see how time makes a difference, look at the chart on page 9 and watch the return column. You'll quickly see that it doesn't take very long for your average earnings to outpace your yearly contribution.

See what's happening? Even though it took nine years for your annual returns to equal your yearly contribution of $6,000, it took only six years more for your returns to add up to double your yearly contribution, more than $12,000 a year. After that, it took only three years for your gain to be $18,000 a year, triple your yearly contribution. Keep in mind that the chart illustrates the magic of compounding in an account earning only an 8 percent average annual return. If you are able to get a higher rate of return, compounding will produce even more dramatic results. If you do not have $6,000 a year to put away, don't be discouraged. It is all the more important for you to start saving now so that time can do as much as possible for you. With as little as $100 a month, you stand a chance of becoming a millionaire. Time is on your side.

Is money always worth so much more if it's left alone for a long time?

Compounding will make your money grow over time. That is why you need to think of your money not only in terms of what it can buy today but also in terms of its potential future value. For example, if you want to spend $20,000 on a trip or a car or some other desirable commodity, try to calculate the cost of that commodity not in today's dollars, but by taking into account the potential future earnings of those dollars. If you invest $20,000 in an account with an annual rate of return of 10 percent and never add another penny, in 20 years that money could easily grow to $135,000. So, as you can see, your car or vacation could really cost you $135,000 in future savings! Sure, inflation will erode the value of your money over time, so go ahead and assume a 3 percent inflation rate each year for 20 years—but a $20,000 purchase is still going to cost you $75,000 (adjusted for inflation).

When you start to see what things truly cost and understand your money's potential value over time, you will begin to understand money. Does this mean that most of your desires are more expensive than they appear to be? Yes. Does it mean that you can't ever buy anything expensive again? No. It means that you will be conscious of the true cost of what you buy, and can make appropriate decisions about whether you can afford to buy it.

My retirement accounts may be all I can rely on in my old age. Should I be conservative and choose only safe investments?

THE BIG BENEFITS OF COMPOUND RETURNS OVER TIME

YEARS IN 401(K) PLAN	ANNUAL CONTRIBUTION	AVERAGE ANNUAL GAIN AT 8% PER YEAR
1	$6,000	$480
2	$6,000	$998
3	$6,000	$1,558
4	$6,000	$2,163
5	$6,000	$2,816
6	$6,000	$3,521
7	$6,000	$4,283
8	$6,000	$5,106
9	$6,000	$5,994* (your gain equals your contribution)
10	$6,000	$6,954
11	$6,000	$7,990
12	$6,000	$9,109
13	$6,000	$10,318
14	$6,000	$11,623
15	$6,000	$13,033* (your gain is more than double your contribution)
16	$6,000	$14,556
17	$6,000	$16,200
18	$6,000	$17,976* (your gain is about three times your contribution)
19	$6,000	$19,894
20	$6,000	$21,966

A conservative investment strategy may sound like a good idea, but it isn't, especially if you are under age 40. In order to keep up with inflation, you must invest your money for growth. The younger you are, the more aggressive you can afford to be with your investment strategy. As a general rule, if you are going to invest your money for at least ten years, invest most of it for growth. Also, remember that in a retirement account, any gains, interest, or dividends are, in most cases, tax-deferred. (In a Roth IRA, in most cases, earnings are tax-free.) What this means is that in a retirement account, your deferred tax money as well as the tax-deferred return it earns go to work for you. This can make a tremendous difference in the accumulation of money.

I'm afraid I'll lose my money if I invest for growth. Is this a valid fear?

When you invest in the stock market, you may see your holdings decline in value from time to time, and you need to feel comfortable with that. If you are going to lie awake at night worrying about your money, then stocks may not be the best investment route for you. But if you invest for the long term and you put the same amount of money into the same investment vehicles every month over time—an investment method called *dollar cost averaging*—in the long run, you probably will not lose money. The concept of dollar cost averaging is explained in greater depth in *Ask Suze . . . About Stocks and Bonds*, but basically it means that you are averaging out the cost of the shares you are purchasing over time. In other words, if you put the same amount of money into the fund each month and the share price fluctuates, you will be buying more shares when the price is lower and fewer shares when the price is higher—you are effectively paying the *average* price. If you are in a good fund for a long time, it's a great opportunity for you when the value of the shares drops, because you can buy shares at "bargain" prices and average down your cost per share.

So it's OK to keep purchasing stocks that drop in value within my retirement account?

If you have at least ten years until you'll need your money, dollar cost averaging into a good mutual fund may be the best thing you can do. You should continue to buy that particular fund if it is not dropping in value at the same time that similar funds are rising in value. If the value of your fund is dropping while similar funds are rising, you need to find out what is going on; this may be a reason to change funds. But if everything similar to your fund is dropping, think of a low share price as a great opportunity to invest for retirement.

Dollar cost averaging makes it sound as though it's better to invest over time rather than all at once. Is that true?

Yes, particularly when you are talking about retirement investing, because you can significantly increase the possibility of future growth. See *Ask Suze . . . About Stocks and Bonds* for an in-depth explanation.

THE MOST POPULAR
RETIREMENT PLANS

The most widely available retirement plans include 401(k)s, 403(b)s, and IRAs. The maximum contributions to these plans change yearly; please see page 111 for details.

401(K)S

What is a 401(k) plan?

A 401(k) is a voluntary retirement plan that companies may offer to their workers. Employees set aside a percentage of their wages before taxes, up to a certain maximum, and invest those funds within the retirement plan. The percentage you can contribute varies from company to company, and the federally mandated yearly maximum may increase over the years, since it is tied to inflation and the consumer price index (CPI). (In 2007, the yearly federal maximum contribution is $15,500 [or $20,500 if you are age 50 or older], and it rises in increments thereafter.) An employer often contributes to its employees' 401(k)s by matching each employee's contribution up to a certain percentage. The contributions and the interest or gains that accrue are not taxed until the funds are withdrawn. There are restrictions on when and how 401(k) funds can be withdrawn.

How does a 401(k) plan work?

You decide how much of your paycheck (up to the maximum allowed) you will contribute to your 401(k) plan. That amount is deducted from your paycheck before taxes are taken out and is deposited automatically into the plan. Normally, you have a choice of several possible mutual funds and other investment vehicles with a variety of levels of potential risk and return. You will be given information about the investment options when you sign up for the 401(k). Many corporations do not allow you to participate in their 401(k) plans until you have worked there for at least one year.

Am I locked in to the investment choices I made when I signed up for my 401(k)?

Not usually, unless you are invested in your company's stock. Typically, if your investment objectives change or you don't like the performance of the funds that you have chosen, it's simple to change your allocations. Most plans allow you to make changes daily, if you want, simply by placing a phone call. Some plans allow changes only once a month, or once a quarter, so be sure to ask. No matter how it is invested, your money, as long as it stays in the plan, will not be taxed. Thus, your investments can grow while you defer taxes, and your total taxable income will be lowered.

Since I am making contributions with pretax dollars, when will I owe taxes on the money in my 401(k)?

Taxes on your 401(k) account are deferred until you withdraw the money at retirement, at which time the money that you withdraw will be taxed as ordinary income. Tax rates on ordinary income currently range from 10 percent to a maximum of 35 percent; please see page 112). Generally, if you withdraw any money before you turn 59½, you will owe a federal tax penalty of 10 percent in addition to the ordinary income tax. Your state may also impose a penalty and state income tax on the withdrawal. Also, when you make withdrawals from a 401(k) plan before age 59½, your company will withhold 20 percent of the amount you have withdrawn for taxes. If you owe more than 20 percent, you will be required to pay it when you file your taxes. If you owe less than the 20 percent, of course, you will get a tax refund.

If I'm not yet 59½, is there any way to avoid that 10 percent early-withdrawal penalty within my 401(k)?

Possibly. It will depend on how old you are and if you are still working for the company that has your 401(k) plan. If you are 55 or older and you leave your employer (retire, quit, or get fired), you can withdraw whatever you want without any penalty from your 401(k). You will still have to pay taxes on the money you withdraw, but you will not have to pay the 10 percent penalty. The penalty also does not apply if you take money from your 401(k) and roll it over into a rollover IRA account. You could also avoid the 10 percent penalty by taking a loan against your 401(k) plan rather than making an actual withdrawal.

Another way to access money in a 401(k) without paying a penalty is to use a payment method called Substantially Equal Periodic Payments (SEPP). To use this method, you will have to withdraw a certain amount of money every year until you are 59½ (or for five years, whichever period is longer). If you started to withdraw money from your 401(k) at age 52, you would need to continue withdrawing money until you are 59½ (seven and a half years being longer than five). But no matter what you do to avoid paying a penalty, you cannot get around paying taxes on the money you withdraw.

How long can I keep money in my 401(k) plan?

There is no fixed time limit. In most cases, the longer you leave your money in a 401(k), the better off you're going to be. Unfortunately, there is an age limit. The IRS says that you must begin to withdraw money from your retirement plans by April 1 of the year after you turn 70½. There is one important exception to this rule: If you are still working for wages when you turn 70½, and your money is in an employer-sponsored plan, such as a 401(k), and you own less than 5 percent of the company you work for, you can leave your money in the plan until April 1 following the calendar year in which you do finally retire. Bear in mind that this exception applies only to employer-sponsored plans, not to plans such as IRAs, which we will discuss later.

What if my employer does not offer a 401(k) or any retirement plan?

It never hurts to ask for one. Get together with your coworkers and ask your employer to establish a 401(k). If you and your colleagues do some preliminary research, you will find there are many mutual fund companies that will be happy to tailor a 401(k) plan for your company. I would start by calling two large money managers, Fidelity Investments, (800) 343-9184; and Vanguard Group, (800) 523-1188. In the meantime—or if your company absolutely will not offer a retirement plan— you can open an individual retirement account or a Roth IRA. (Even if you participate in a company 401(k), you can still open an IRA, though you may not be able to deduct your contributions.)

I'm in a 401(k) plan at work and make about $200,000 a year, but my employer will not let me contribute as much to my 401(k) as other employees are allowed to. Why?

You are what the government considers a "highly compensated employee"—someone who makes at least $100,000 a year as of the year 2007 or owns 5 percent or more of a company. To meet government rules, your employer may not be able to allow you to contribute the maximum amount allowed. That is because the government doesn't want the amount of money contributed to the plan by highly compensated employees to be much larger than the amount contributed by employees who aren't paid as well. A plan is considered "top-heavy" if higher-paid employees contribute substantially more than lower-paid employees. If lower-paid employees are contributing very little to the 401(k), then you, as a highly compensated employee, may not be able to contribute anything at all.

One of the investment options in my 401(k) is my company's stock. Should I invest in that?

Generally, I think it is OK to invest in your employer's stock, as long as you thoroughly diversify your investments—in other words, as long as you don't invest all, or even much, of your 401(k) money in your company's stock. You already have a lot invested in your company—your job and job security—and even very solid companies can experience frightening declines in the value of their stock, for a variety of reasons. Putting aside the disaster for Enron employees who had much of their retirement savings in company stock that plunged in 2001–2002, consider this example: In 2000, Microsoft employees watched *their* stock drop from $120 a share to $45 a share. As bad as that sounds for outside shareholders, try to imagine the horror felt by employees who had invested their retirement savings in their company stock. Not to mention those employees who were retiring that year and were planning to live off their 401(k)s—not a nice situation. So don't put all your eggs in one basket. My recommendation is to have no more than 4 to 10 percent of your total assets invested in company stock.

I'm not crazy about the investment options for my 401(k). Can I do anything about it?

Possibly. Many employers allow what is known as a partial rollover. You take a percentage of the money that is in your 401(k) (usually no more than 50 percent is allowed), and you transfer it into another retirement account (held in your name by another custodian, such as a bank or a brokerage firm). Not all companies allow partial rollovers, but many do.

My company says it will match my 401(k) contributions. What does that mean?

It means just what it says—your company will match the contributions you make to your 401(k) plan by putting money into your plan. An employer's contribution is usually set by a formula and has a maximum. For instance, for every dollar you put into your 401(k) plan, your employer might give you 50 cents, up to a certain percentage of what you put in. Some generous employers will match any percentage of your contributions dollar for dollar. If your employer does match any percentage of your 401(k) contributions, you cannot afford to pass this up—this is free money. Think about it—if your employer matches 50 cents on the dollar, for every dollar it matches you are essentially getting an automatic 50 percent return on that money.

I have credit card debt. Should I continue to participate in a 401(k)?

Regardless of your financial situation, it depends on if your employer provides any matching contributions. That's free money that you don't want to pass up. In many plans, the employer will match your contributions up to a certain dollar limit. In that case, it makes sense for you to contribute up to that limit. Then after you've maxed out on the employer match, you can make a decision about whether to continue with your contributions. You need to decide if the rate of return on your 401(k) and the value of your contribution being tax-free outweigh the benefit of paying off the credit card debt. If the interest rate on your credit card balance is higher than what you can earn on your 401(k), then you might want to temporarily suspend those extra contributions and pay off the debt. If you have a zero percent interest rate on your credit card and are doing well in your 401(k) plan, don't stop contributing.

What does it mean to be vested in my 401(k) plan?

Being vested means you have the right to take the amount of money that your employer contributed to your retirement account, as well as your own contributions, with you if you leave the company. Until you are vested, even though your employer's money is in your retirement account, it is not yours if you leave your job. This way a company protects itself against giving money to employees who may leave right away. (Not only would they lose you—they'd lose their money as well.) Vesting entices workers to stay with a company longer to get access to money the company has put in their retirement accounts. Regardless, some companies allow you to vest in your 401(k) plan right away; others make you wait as long as from three to seven years.

I am not yet vested in my 401(k) account, but I want to leave to work for another company. Does that mean I lose all the money I contributed to my 401(k)?

Absolutely not. When you leave a job, for any reason, you can always take your own 401(k) contributions with you.

My company does a four-year vesting, based on 25 percent a year. What does that mean?

Some companies phase in vesting rights, such as 25 percent the first year, 50 percent the second year, 75 percent the third year, and 100 percent the fourth year. Let's say you have been working for a company with this type of plan for almost two years. Each month, you have been contributing $300 of your salary to your 401(k), and your company has been contributing $100. If you leave one month before your second anniversary with the company, then, in addition to your own contributions, you will be entitled to 25 percent of the company's contributions, or about $575, plus gains (or losses) on that money. If you could wait to leave until after your second anniversary, a month later, you would be 50 percent vested, and entitled to half of what your company has contributed over the two years: $1,200, plus gains or losses.

If I leave the company where I currently have my 401(k) plan, do I have to take my money out of that plan?

It depends on the company. Many employers will allow you to leave money in their 401(k) plans. Others will require you to roll it over.

Are there benefits to leaving money in a 401(k) plan after I retire?

If you are 55 or older in the year you retire, the big advantage of leaving some or all of your retirement funds in a company plan is that you can make withdrawals as often and in any amount you want without paying a penalty. Also, most company plans do not charge fees or commissions for managing your money.

Is there a downside to leaving my retirement money invested in a 401(k) plan when I retire?

It depends on your company plan. Your money might earn more elsewhere. Often there are a limited number of investment options in a 401(k) plan, and some plans limit you to making investment changes once a quarter, although this is not as common a restriction as it used to be. Some plans require you to fill out change forms personally rather than simply order changes over the telephone, and if your company does not have an automated system for processing transfers, it could take three to six weeks to put any of your changes into effect, which could wind up costing you a lot of money. Finally, you generally don't get professional advice in your company's retirement plan, which means that you are solely responsible for figuring out how to invest your money. Also, if you die with money in the plan, the plan may restrict the options your beneficiary has.

My company offers a Roth 401(k). How is that different from my traditional 401(k)?

Consider yourself lucky; as of early 2007, not many employers offered Roth 401(k)s, though that should change thanks to congressional legislation that encourages companies to offer this option. With a Roth 401(k), you get no up-front tax break on your contributions; just like a Roth IRA (see page 39), the money you invest is after-tax. But the big payoff is that when you retire, all your withdrawals will be 100 percent tax-free. Remember, with a traditional 401(k), all withdrawals are taxed at your ordinary income-tax rate. My general advice is that if you have at least 10 years until retirement, it makes a lot of sense to opt for a Roth 401(k) if your company offers it.

403(B) PLANS

Who can invest in a 403(b) plan?

Employees of nonprofit organizations—for example, some hospitals, universities, and charitable organizations—generally have 403(b) plans available to them.

What's the difference between a 401(k) and a 403(b)?

From your perspective as an investor, they work almost identically, and when I refer to 401(k) plans in this book, you can assume that what I'm saying applies to 403(b) plans as well. The main difference is that in some 403(b)s, you cannot change the amount of money that you put in every month. You must decide once, at the beginning of the year. Many 403(b) plans don't offer as many investment choices as 401(k)s—most 403(b)s offer only mutual funds and annuities—but, again, that depends on where you work. Another difference is that long-term employees using 403(b) plans can often do what's called a "catch-up election," which allows them to contribute more than the yearly maximum allowed if they have more than fifteen years of service (subject to certain requirements). If you have a choice between a 401(k) and a 403(b), check them both out carefully. You will probably find that the 401(k) is a better deal. However, if all you have is a 403(b) at your disposal, use it.

Is a 403(b) a qualified plan?

Not technically, but it functions like one. When it comes time to withdraw your money, a 403(b) plan is not eligible for ten-year averaging or capital-gains taxation, as qualified plans are. But very few individuals qualify for those breaks anyway and, other than that, a 403(b) behaves like a qualified plan.

What is a TSA?

TSA stands for tax-sheltered annuity; it is a form of 403(b) plan. It invests the retirement contributions in an annuity with an insurance company. A TSA is also sometimes knows as a TDA, or tax-deferred annuity.

What is a 457 plan?

This is a voluntary, nonqualified retirement plan typically offered to employees of state and local government agencies. 457 plans may also be offered to employees of nongovernmental tax-exempt or nonprofit organizations, but provisions may differ from those listed here. A government-sponsored 457 plan usually allows participants to annually defer up to $15,500 in wages, or $20,000 if you are age 50 or older (for the year 2007); as with 401(k)s and 403(b)s, these amounts are scheduled to increase annually. Please see page 111. Your contributions and earnings will not be taxed until you begin to withdraw the funds. A government-sponsored 457 plan is different from a 401(k) or a 403(b) plan in that there is no minimum retirement age and no 10 percent federal penalty for early withdrawal of funds. These plans also contain a provision allowing, under certain conditions, rollover of assets from government-sponsored 457 plans into other retirement plans, such as IRAs, 401(k)s, 403(b)s, and other 457s. Also, in government-sponsored 457 plans a special catch-up rule applies if you are three or fewer years away from retirement, letting you contribute up to twice the annual maximum otherwise in effect in any given year.

THE NOT-SO-WELL-KNOWN RETIREMENT PLANS

What is a defined-benefit pension plan?

A defined-benefit pension plan is a qualified retirement plan that promises to pay a specific amount to an employee who retires after a certain number of years. The benefit might be an exact dollar amount, for example, $4,000 per month. More common, the benefit might be determined by a formula that takes into account factors such as salary and length of employment with the company. For example, you might receive a monthly payment of 1 percent of your average salary during the last five years of employment for every year of service with your employer.

A defined-benefit pension plan is funded by the employer that creates it, not by the employees. The money that is held within a defined-benefit plan is not allocated to individual accounts; it is kept in one big account with all the money for all the employees. Money from this plan is usually not available for withdrawal until you reach retirement age, at which time you can receive it as a lump-sum payment, if your plan allows it, or as a lifetime annuity. If you take the money as an annuity, you won't be able to roll it over into an IRA and continue to defer taxes, which you can do if you take your retirement funds as a lump sum. So make sure you think through the tax implications if you have a choice of how to receive the benefit. Also, though you have been promised a defined benefit when you retire, if you leave that job or retire before the set retirement date, your benefits will be redefined. The bottom line is that the company is responsible for funding the plan, and it is responsible for giving the full benefit that has been defined. By law, it cannot fall short of that goal.

What is a target-benefit plan?

This qualified retirement plan works somewhat like a defined-benefit plan, except that the employees all have separate accounts. In this plan the benefit is defined as a target to be met at the time of retirement. So while a defined-benefit plan guarantees a specific retirement benefit, the target-benefit just estimates and hopes to come close to the target. When the plan is opened up, the employer sets a benefit goal and estimates (with the help of actuaries) how much money will need to be invested each year to reach it. Once this formula has been set, it is frozen. If the investment performance of this formula falls short, then you lose—you won't get the target benefit. If the account performs beyond expectations, however, any increase in benefit must also be passed on to the employees.

What is a defined-contribution plan?

Examples of defined-contribution plans include 401(k) plans, 403(b) plans, employee stock ownership plans, and profit-sharing plans. They are qualified retirement plans in which a certain amount or percentage of money is set aside every year for the employee's benefit. Simply put, the contribution is defined, but the benefit isn't; there is no way to know how much money the employee will get at retirement. The contributions in this plan may come from the employees, the employer, or both. In contrast to defined-benefit accounts, the funds of a defined-contribution plan are held in the employee's name. Sometimes the amount set aside is a set percentage of your annual salary. These contributions are generally invested on your behalf, and you will ultimately receive the balance—the contributions plus or minus any investment gains or losses. That means that the value of your retirement account will fluctuate with the value of your investments. There are restrictions on withdrawing these funds before retirement age.

What is a profit-sharing plan?

This is a retirement plan that usually, but not always, does just what the name suggests. In a profit-sharing plan, a company uses its profits to fund a qualified retirement plan for its employees. But the company has a lot of leeway. From year to year, it does not have to contribute to the plan, even when there are profits to share. On the other hand, it may decide to contribute to the plan even if there are no profits that year. Yes, you heard right—in a profit-sharing plan, the employer has the discretion to contribute or not, regardless of profitability. When the employer does contribute, the contribution formula is based on your compensation. As of the year 2007 (the latest available as of this writing), the contribution could be no more than 25 percent of your pay, up to a maximum eligible income of $225,000. The maximum dollar amount that could be contributed as of 2007 was $45,000. Percentages and maximum amounts may increase in years to come.

What is a money-purchase pension plan?

This is a qualified retirement plan that is similar to a profit-sharing plan, but because the frequency and amount of the employer's contributions are predetermined, I like this plan much better. In a money-purchase plan, the employer promises to contribute a fixed percentage of your annual salary, including any bonuses, each year, and that cannot change. Until 2002, another benefit of a money-purchase plan was that the contribution limits were higher than in a profit-sharing plan, but now the limits are the same: In 2007, the contribution could not be more than 25 percent of your pay, up to a maximum eligible income of $225,000 and a maximum dollar amount of $45,000. Percentages and maximum amounts may increase in years to come.

What is a stock bonus plan?

This qualified retirement plan works very much like a profit-sharing plan. The only difference is that the employer makes its contributions in the form of company stock instead of cash.

INDIVIDUAL RETIREMENT ACCOUNTS (IRAS)

The following section is devoted to traditional IRAs; it is followed by a section on Roth IRAs. Many of the features of a traditional IRA and a Roth IRA are the same. Where features are identical, you will see the designation T/R, for traditional/Roth. Please be sure to look at both sections.

What is a traditional IRA?

A traditional Individual Retirement Account allows you to

establish your own tax-deferred savings-and-investment account outside the auspices of an employer. In the years 2006 and 2007, you can contribute up to $4,000 to your IRA and, if you are married, you can contribute up to $4,000 more for a non-working spouse. (The maximum contribution rises to $5,000 in 2008 and rises again in following years. Please see page 111.) People age 50 and older can contribute an additional $1,000 a year.

If you meet certain guidelines, you can deduct your annual IRA contribution from your income, thereby reducing the taxes that you owe that year. Once it is deposited in an IRA account, the money will grow tax-deferred until you withdraw it, at which time you will pay ordinary income tax on it.

What are the features and advantages of a traditional IRA?

A traditional IRA allows you to take a current-year tax deduction for your contribution, provided you meet the tax-law qualifications set forth by the IRS. If you are also covered by an employer-sponsored retirement plan like a 401(k), you might not be able to even partially deduct your contribution. If you do qualify for the deduction, you can subtract the amount of your contribution from your taxable income. Let's say you earn $28,000 a year and you qualify for the deduction. In 2007, you can contribute $4,000 to a traditional IRA and pay taxes on only $24,000 of your income. In addition to that terrific tax break, the money in the IRA—both your contributions and any income they earn—grows tax-deferred until you actually withdraw it. Also, when you withdraw money from an IRA you do not have to withhold 20 percent of the amount for taxes, which is required when you take money out of a 401(k) plan.

If I do not work, can I open and contribute to a traditional IRA?

Only those who have *earned* income or alimony can contribute to an IRA. Earned income is defined as wages, commissions, bonuses, tips, self-employment income, and fees for professional services. You *cannot* count Social Security, pension or annuity payments, interest or dividend income, income from real estate, or deferred compensation. If *all* of your income is derived from one or more of those nonearned sources, you won't be able to put any money in an IRA, unless your spouse has earned income.

Can someone give me the money to open a T/R IRA?

Yes, as long as you are otherwise earning at least the same amount of money as wages or other taxable compensation. In other words, if you make $4,000 in wages in the year 2007 and your parents want to give you up to $4,000 to contribute to an IRA, that's OK. But if you were not employed or did not earn at least $4,000, you couldn't put the full gift into an IRA.

When I do take money out of my traditional IRA, what do I need to know?

When you withdraw money from your IRA, it will be taxed as ordinary income in the year of the withdrawal. Generally, you cannot make a withdrawal from a traditional IRA until you are 59½ without paying a 10 percent federal penalty on the amount you withdraw. On the other hand, you *must* start taking withdrawals from your IRA on April 1 after the year in which you turn 70½. If you don't begin withdrawing money by then, you will have to pay a 50 percent annual penalty on the amount of money that was supposed to be withdrawn!

Are there any exceptions to the 10 percent early-withdrawal penalty for a T/R IRA besides being 59½ years of age or older?

Yes, there are exceptions. But be aware that even if you avoid paying a 10 percent penalty for early withdrawal, you will still have to pay income taxes on that money (or, in the case of a Roth, on the earnings portion of that money). You will not have to pay the penalty if:

1. *You suffered a disability.* For you to avoid the 10 percent penalty under this exception, you must prove that you cannot do any activity that would allow you to earn a living. A doctor is going to have to verify that you are seriously disabled and are expected to stay that way for a long time—possibly indefinitely—for this exception to fly.

2. *You have died.* When your beneficiaries inherit your IRA and start to take out the money, regardless of their age, they will not have to pay a penalty. However, they will have to pay taxes.

3. *You have incurred great medical expenses.* If you have medical bills that will not be covered or reimbursed by your insurance company, and those expenses exceed 7.5 percent of your adjusted gross income, you may qualify for this exception.

4. *You are a first-time home buyer.* If you are planning to build, rebuild, or buy a house as a primary residence, you might be able to withdraw a maximum of $10,000 from your IRA without incurring a 10 percent penalty. This money can be used for a home for anyone in your family—you, your parents, your grandparents, your children, or your grandchildren. This includes your spouse's side of the family as well.

There is a time frame on this withdrawal that you need to be aware of. You must use the money for a viable expense within 120 days of withdrawing it from your account. The money has to be spent on what the IRS considers valid expenses of buying or building a home, such as closing costs, etc. Even though you are exempt from paying the early-withdrawal penalty, you will still have to pay income taxes on this money. "First-time homebuyer," by the way, does not mean first time ever. It simply means that you have not owned a home in the previous two years. So if you owned a home, sold it, and now, two years later, you want to buy another home, you can qualify for this exception.

5. *You need money to pay for college.* You or anyone in your family can use any of the money in your IRA to help pay for secondary, undergraduate, or graduate education. The money can be used for a variety of education expenses, including room and board (for students attending school at least half-time), books, supplies, tuition, and equipment needed for classes. Again, please note: You will avoid the early-withdrawal penalty here, but you will still owe taxes.

6. You need to pay for health insurance. If you need money to pay for medical insurance premiums for you, your spouse, or your dependents, and you meet all of the following criteria, you can take money out of your IRA and not have to pay the early-withdrawal penalty.

- You are not employed because you lost your job.
- You have received unemployment compensation for at least 12 consecutive weeks.

- The money will be withdrawn from your IRA in the same calendar year you received unemployment.

If you do get another job, the money must be withdrawn from the IRA within 60 days of the date you were hired.

7. *You are using a technique known as substantially equal periodic payments, or SEPP.* If you are younger than 59½ and you need to get money out of a retirement account, such as a traditional IRA, and you want to avoid the 10 percent early-withdrawal penalty, you might consider making substantially equal periodic payments. Essentially, this means making regular withdrawals from your IRA until you are of retirement age (59½) or for at least five years, whichever is longer.

If I decide to use the SEPP method, how do I figure out how much my payments would be each year?
The three methods of calculation you (and the IRS) can use to determine the amount of your substantially equal periodic payments are based on life expectancy, amortization, and annuity. How much you must withdraw each month depends on the method you use; each method applies a different formula to several factors, including your life expectancy and the estimated rate of return on your investment. In most cases, people use the amortization method, because it's easier, but often the annuity method will give them the most income. Make this decision carefully—I recommend getting help from a CPA or professional financial adviser well versed in SEPP— because once you choose your method and start receiving SEPP payments, you cannot change it. Make sure the firm that calculates your SEPP states on company letterhead (not

just the adviser's personal letterhead) that the company will be responsible for calculating your substantially equal periodic payments, and that it will be responsible for any mistakes and penalties.

What are the pitfalls of withdrawing money using substantially equal periodic payments?

There are a couple tricky things to keep in mind when withdrawing money this way. First, under the amortization method, you have to take out the same amount of money every month, or if you prefer annual withdrawals, they must be identical from year to year. If you aren't careful, and if you don't take the correct amount of money, which is set according to IRS rules, you could be vulnerable to penalties later. Please note: Some investments, such as annuities, meet the rules of SEPP even though the first year's distribution will vary from that of other years.

Does it matter how my retirement account is invested during the time I am taking SEPP?

Because the way in which your money is invested is significant under SEPP, whether or not you will need to make changes depends on how you are invested. As a general rule, when investing for SEPP, invest at least 80 percent of your funds for income instead of growth. Over the five years or more that you are taking SEPP withdrawals, you don't want to risk the stock market—and your income—dropping, potentially forcing you to make withdrawals from your principal. When the SEPP period is over, you can again invest for growth.

How do I figure out if I can contribute to a traditional IRA and deduct the amount of my contribution from my income for tax purposes?

Whether or not you can deduct your contribution to a traditional IRA depends on whether you are covered by a qualifying employer-sponsored retirement plan such as a 401(k) plan and what your filing status and income are in the taxable year. If you are covered by a retirement plan at work, you still may be able to deduct all or part of your IRA contribution.

What are the income limits on deducting contributions to a traditional IRA?

Please note: The full deductibility of the yearly contribution limit in an IRA is phased out from 100 percent deductible to zero percent after you have reached the income limitations. The phase-out income ranges rise each year; in 2007, the phase-out range is $50,000 to $60,000 for single taxpayers and $80,000 to $100,000 for married taxpayers filing jointly. If you are married and you make more than the yearly limit, you may still contribute to a traditional IRA, but you won't be able to take the deduction.

The chart on page 33 is a list of income ranges for use in determining the amount of an IRA contribution that can be deducted. See page 39 to learn how to calculate modified adjusted gross income.

If you earn too much to take the deduction, you may still qualify for a Roth IRA, which we will discuss in detail later in the chapter.

My income falls in the middle of the phase-out range. How do I figure out what portion of my traditional IRA contribution is tax-deductible?

You use a simple formula based on your income level and marital status. Basically, you subtract your modified adjusted gross income from the largest figure for the relevant tax year, then multiply the difference by 0.20; that is how much money you will be able to deduct. Here's an example: Let's say that you are single and have a modified adjusted gross income of $50,000 in the year 2007. The maximum figure for your phase-out range in 2007 is $60,000. So you subtract $50,000 from $60,000 and get $10,000. Now you multiply $10,000 by 0.20 and you'll see that you can deduct $2,000 of your $4,000 IRA contribution that year.

I am covered by a pension plan, but my spouse doesn't work. Can we deduct her contribution if we are within the income limits?

In that case, if you are covered by a pension plan and have a spouse who is not, the income limits for the non-covered spouse's IRA deductibility rise. If your modified adjusted gross income as a married couple filing jointly is less than $150,000, you can take a full deduction on a traditional IRA contribution for a nonworking spouse during that year. If your income is more than $160,000, you cannot deduct a traditional IRA contribution for your nonworking spouse at all. Of course, if you are not an active participant in an employer's retirement plan, you can always deduct a traditional IRA contribution from your taxes. Still, you might be better off with a Roth IRA if you qualify.

INCOME LIMITS TO DEDUCT YOUR IRA CONTRIBUTIONS

SINGLE

YEAR	MODIFIED ADJUSTED GROSS INCOME PHASE-OUT RANGE
2007	$50,000–$60,000
2008 onward	Indexed to inflation

MARRIED, FILING JOINTLY

YEAR	MODIFIED ADJUSTED GROSS INCOME PHASE-OUT RANGE
2007	$80,000–$100,000
2008 onward	Indexed to inflation

I have a 401(k) plan, so I don't qualify for a tax deduction for an IRA. Does that disqualify my spouse as well?
Keep in mind that one spouse is not considered to be covered by a pension plan just because the other spouse is. A spouse without a qualified pension plan can make a fully deductible IRA contribution as long as the couple's modified adjusted gross income does not exceed $150,000.

Where can I open up a T/R IRA account?
You can open an IRA account at many institutions: a full-service or discount brokerage firm, a mutual-fund company, an insurance company, a bank, or a credit union.

What can I invest in within my T/R IRA?
Once you open your account, you can invest it in a variety of ways—you can put your money in stocks and mutual funds, high-interest savings accounts, annuities, bonds, etc. Your selection will depend on what the firm you opened your IRA with offers, which, depending on the company, can restrict your options in ways you hadn't planned. For this reason, I always suggest opening an IRA at a company that offers you a variety of investments at a good cost, such as discount brokerage firms like Muriel Siebert or Ameritrade.

What is the deadline for opening a T/R IRA for a specific tax year?
The deadline for opening an IRA for a given tax year is April

15 of the following calendar year. In other words, you can open up an IRA on April 15, 2008, and it will apply to the tax year 2007. Many people are aware of this deadline and don't open their IRA until April of the year *after* they could have done so. This is a mistake. For the tax year 2007, for example, you have the right to put $4,000 in your IRA on January 1, 2007. But most people wait until April 2008 to do so, thereby losing more than a year's worth of tax-deferred or tax-free compounding earnings.

Does it make a difference when I invest my T/R IRA contribution?

Waiting to invest almost always costs you. If you wait until the following tax year to make a contribution, you may be losing money. Remember the power of compounding gains. If you possibly can, put that money away at the beginning of the year rather than at the tax deadline. If you invest $4,000 in January of 2007, for example, and that money sits in your IRA earning an 8 percent return, by the time April 15 of the 2008 tax year comes along, you would have an extra $360 in the account.

Now look at the big picture. If you put away the maximum contribution allowed each year for the next 25 years, and this money earns an 8 percent average annual return, after 25 years of putting this contribution in every January like clockwork, you would have approximately $340,000 in your IRA. If instead you waited until April of the following year to make this contribution, you'd have about $300,000, a potential loss of $40,000.

If you don't have the money at the beginning of the year or can't make the investment all at once, put whatever you can each month into your IRA. You will still come out better than if you wait to do it in one lump sum.

If I have a 401(k) plan at work, can I also have a T/R IRA?

Yes, you can put money into both a 401(k) and an IRA but, depending on your income level and your tax filing status, you may not be able to take the full tax deduction of the traditional IRA. If you qualify for a Roth, that's a better investment.

If I am putting as much money into my 401(k) plan as my employer allows, should I bother getting a T/R IRA?

Yes, and the reason is very straightforward: If you give up a little bit of money now, you will have a lot more to live on after you retire. Every extra dollar that you save, whether taxed, tax-deferred, or tax-free, and invest today instead of spending will grow exponentially over time. However, if you can qualify for a Roth IRA, you would be better off opening up a Roth than a traditional IRA.

Can I have more than one T/R IRA?

Absolutely. You can invest in as many IRAs as you want, but you can't contribute more than the current annual maximum each year to all your IRAs. This means that if you have five IRAs in the year 2007, you can put $800 in each—you can divvy up the $4,000 among the accounts any way you like.

Is there an advantage to having more than one T/R IRA account?

In most cases there is actually a disadvantage to having more than one. You see, most IRAs charge a yearly fee. That fee can run anywhere from $25 to $50. That may not seem like a lot of money, but it is when you look at it in terms of percentages. If you are paying $30 a year for an IRA, and all you have in the account is $300, you are paying 10 percent of the account value just for the custodial fee. This means that even if your investment went up 10 percent that year, all you did was break even. However, if you had all your 2007 contribution of $4,000 in just one account and the fee was $30, well, that's not so bad—less than 1 percent of the account value. So if your investment within the IRA went up 10 percent, after the custodial fee (assuming it is deducted from the IRA account itself) you still would have made about 9 percent on your money that year.

Does every brokerage firm charge a fee?
No, some do not. Please shop around for an IRA brokerage firm.

Are the custodial fees you pay for a T/R IRA tax-deductible?
Theoretically, yes. If you pay these fees with funds outside of your IRA, if you itemize deductions on your return, and if the fees and other miscellaneous itemized deductions total more than 2 percent of your adjusted gross income, the fees are tax-deductible. In practice, most people have custodial fees deducted right from the IRA account, in which case they are not tax-deductible.

Once I've opened a T/R IRA, am I obligated to contribute the maximum amount allowed each year?
No. You can open an IRA and invest the maximum allowed in the year you open it and then never contribute another penny to it. You also may contribute less than the maximum to it in any given year. But I think you should make funding your IRA to the maximum each year a priority, particularly if you are not covered by another type of retirement plan.

What is the difference in monetary terms between a 401(k) plan and a T/R IRA?

In 2007, the difference amounts to about $11,550 a year—and more if you're age 50 or older. The maximum amount you can put into an IRA in 2007 is $4,000—not much to hope to retire on. In a 401(k), qualified employees are allowed to contribute up to $15,500 a year, or $20,500 if they are age 50 or older. That difference should be a big incentive to push your employer to sponsor a retirement plan.

Another difference is the protection that a 401(k) plan has from creditors. (The same goes for 403(b) or Keogh plans.) The Employee Retirement Income Security Act (ERISA) protects assets in these qualified, tax-deferred retirement plans from the claims of the participant's creditors. IRAs do not have federal protection against the claims of creditors (though many states provide protection), so if you get into trouble with debt, you may lose your retirement savings.

When I go to take money out of my IRA, can I take it out in stock? Or do I have to sell my stock and take it out in cash?

You can take it out in stock if you want to. Say you want to withdraw $15,000. You can withdraw it in cash, or in $15,000 of stock. If you do this, you will pay ordinary income taxes on the value of the stock on the day it was withdrawn (plus a 10 percent penalty if you are not at least 59½). If you later sell the stock at an increased value, you will owe taxes on that gain as well.

ROTH IRAS

Roth IRAs were created by an act of Congress in 1996. With a Roth IRA, you may not deduct your contribution, but your contributions can grow income tax–free. When you withdraw money from a Roth IRA at retirement, you will not owe any taxes on that money, no matter how much the money has grown in value, provided you have followed IRS guidelines. What few people seem to realize is that in a contributory, or non-tax-deferred, Roth IRA, you can withdraw your own contributions at any time without penalties or taxes, regardless of your age and how long the money has been in the Roth. Any gains your contributions earn, however, must stay in the Roth IRA until you have turned 59½ *and* you've held your account for more than five years before you can withdraw them without taxes or penalties. Earnings from Roth IRA contributions *can* be withdrawn penalty-free if you become disabled or die.

What are the Roth's income limitations?
Single taxpayers whose modified adjusted gross income (MAGI) is less than $99,000 per year and married couples who have a combined annual MAGI of less than $156,000 can contribute up to $4,000 each (or $5,000 if they are 50 or over). Your eligibility to contribute the full $4,000 (or $5,000 if you are over 50) is phased out between $99,000 and $114,000 for single taxpayers and between $156,000 and $166,000 for married taxpayers filing jointly. After those amounts, you are not eligible for a Roth IRA.

What exactly is modified adjusted gross income?
Modified adjusted gross income, or MAGI, is determined by taking your adjusted gross income (AGI) and adding back a

variety of items. Adjusted gross income is defined as your total taxable income minus certain expenses, such as qualified plan contributions, IRA contributions, and alimony payments. To figure out your MAGI, take your AGI and add back:

- Income from U.S. savings bonds used for higher-education expenses;
- Any expenses your employer paid for you to adopt a child;
- Foreign earned income and payments received for foreign housing;
- Any deductions claimed on regular IRA contributions;
- Any deductions taken for interest on an education loan.

What are the advantages of a Roth IRA over a traditional IRA?

There are several. First, the Roth potentially allows you to amass a lot over the long term in exchange for not taking a tax deduction now. If, from ages 21 to 30, you invested $4,000 in a Roth IRA averaging a yearly return of about 8 percent and never added another penny, you would have about $606,000 at age 59½, income tax–free. That's a huge difference from a traditional IRA, on which you or your beneficiaries would eventually have to pay income taxes on that same sum. To have tax-free access to that Roth money, you simply give up the tax deduction that a traditional IRA offers you on your contributions—at a time when you may be in a pretty low income-tax bracket anyway.

Second, if you have a traditional IRA and you die, your spouse is the only person allowed to take over the IRA as a retirement account. Assuming that you haven't already started to withdraw the money, your surviving spouse can use the tax-deferral strategies of the traditional IRA until he or she really needs the money or turns 70½. But if you are not married, the named beneficiary on a traditional IRA will be required to start making withdrawals in the year after you die and will have to continue making them through his or her life—or until the account is cleaned out, which usually comes first. This presents a significant tax burden to the beneficiary. With a Roth IRA, a beneficiary will inherit the money free and clear of income taxes (as long as distribution started more than five years after the opening of the account). Estate taxes, if any, still apply.

Another major advantage of the Roth IRA is that you do not have to begin taking withdrawals at age 70½, as you do with a traditional IRA. If you don't really need the money but are forced to begin withdrawing money from a traditional IRA anyway, it will only increase your adjusted gross income—and thus your income taxes.

But the two main reasons Roth IRAs are so popular is that the earnings are tax-free instead of tax-deferred, and you can take out your original contributions anytime you want, regardless of your age, without taxes or penalties.

Can I have a Roth IRA if I already have a 401(k)?
Yes, as long as you meet the income qualifications.

I already have a 401(k). Are there drawbacks to having a traditional IRA vs. a Roth IRA?
There may be. Because you already have a 401(k), you can't take any tax deductions on traditional IRA contributions if you earn more than the IRA income limit (see the chart on page 33). Plus, you will still have to pay ordinary income tax on the growth of this money when you withdraw it. With a Roth IRA, you can't deduct your contributions either, but your withdrawals after the age of 59½ will be income tax–free.

If I qualify for both a Roth IRA and my company's 401(k), which should I invest in first?

Which you invest in first depends on four factors: (1) whether your employer matches your contributions to your 401(k); (2) the investment options your 401(k) plan offers; (3) your current tax bracket; and (4) whether you foresee needing the money in your retirement plan before turning 59½. If your company matches your 401(k) contribution, you cannot—and I stress, you *cannot*—pass that up. So fund your 401(k) at least up to the limit of your employer's matching contribution. After getting the maximum match on your 401(k), I would suggest funding a Roth IRA, and then, if there's anything left, contributing whatever more you can to your 401(k). If your tax bracket is high and/or you may need to withdraw money before 59½, please see a tax professional.

Can I have a Roth IRA and a traditional IRA at the same time?

Sure. Remember, though, that you can contribute only the maximum amount allowed in total each year to your IRAs, no matter how many you have or what kinds they are.

I'm already contributing the maximum allowable amount to my pension plan at work. I make too much money to qualify for a traditional IRA or a Roth IRA. Is there any other type of retirement account I can look into?

You can open a nondeductible IRA, which is just like a traditional IRA except that you can't deduct your contributions. Go ahead and do this. Even though you won't be able to deduct your contributions, your money will still grow tax-deferred.

*If I have a few separate Roth IRAs and I want to with-
draw some of my money but am not yet 59½, does it
matter which Roth I tap into?*

For tax purposes, the IRS aggregates all your Roth IRAs and
considers them one account. Also, once you begin to withdraw
money from these accounts, your contributions are considered
to be the first withdrawals that you make. So if you have contributed, say, $4,000 into each of two different Roth IRAs
and one has grown to $8,000 and the other to $6,700, you do
not have to withdraw $4,000 from each account. You can close
out the $8,000 account.

Is there anyone who shouldn't have a Roth IRA?

In my opinion, there is only one situation in which it might
make sense to have a traditional IRA rather than a Roth IRA.
If you are in a high tax bracket during the years you will be
making your contributions, really need the tax write-off that
the traditional IRA will give you, *and* know, without a shadow
of a doubt, that you will be in a very low tax bracket when you
take this money out—then, yes, a traditional IRA might be
better than a Roth. But it's tricky to predict the tax bracket
you'll be in at retirement. In most cases, I would opt for the
Roth IRA.

*Why do you so strongly prefer Roth IRAs to traditional
IRAs?*

The Roth IRA protects you from some future uncertainties.
For example, say an unforeseen expense comes up and you
need money before you turn 59½. A Roth IRA allows you to
access your contributions without taxes or penalties, no matter
what your age or how long your money has been in the
account. It's also hard to be sure what tax bracket you will be

in when you make your withdrawals. With the Roth IRA, your money is protected from future taxes—you paid them at the time of deposit and won't have to pay them at withdrawal. You may not know, in many cases, if you will even need to use the money in your Roth IRA. If you don't, you can leave the Roth IRA to your beneficiaries income tax–free as well. This makes a big difference. Say you have $300,000 in a traditional IRA when you retire. You will owe taxes on that money at whatever tax rates are in effect at the time you go to withdraw it. Who can say how much of that $300,000 you will be able to keep? With a Roth IRA, that is not a problem—income taxes do not affect you if all requirements are met.

The bottom line: With a Roth IRA, you know exactly how much money you will have when you retire. Income taxes will not deplete your account.

ROTH CONVERSIONS

What is a Roth conversion?
Starting in the late 90s, people who had traditional IRAs were allowed to convert them into Roth IRAs. The process came to be known as a Roth conversion. Conversions are not subject to early-withdrawal penalties, but are subject to ordinary income tax.

Can anyone transfer or convert money from a traditional IRA to a Roth IRA?
Not yet. As of 2007, to convert any or all of a traditional IRA to a Roth IRA, your annual modified adjusted gross income (MAGI) must not exceed $100,000 in the year that you are making the conversion; if you are married and filing a joint

return, unfortunately, your joint MAGI must also not exceed $100,000. (This is one instance where being married truly penalizes you.) If you and your spouse have lived apart for a full year and filed separate returns, however, you might qualify. But thanks to recent legislation, that $100,000 income restriction will be lifted, starting in 2010.

Can I convert my traditional IRA to a Roth anytime I want?

The traditional IRA money must be withdrawn by December 31 of the year in which you are converting and deposited within the Roth IRA within 60 days. All withdrawals and transfers should be done from trustee to trustee; you should not handle the money yourself.

Can you convert just some of a traditional IRA, or do you have to convert the whole thing?

It's common for people to think that they have to convert all the funds in a traditional IRA, but that's not the case. You can convert any amount of money you want as long you meet the income requirement—that is, your modified adjusted gross income is not greater than $100,000—in the year you convert.

Can I convert a 401(k) account to a Roth IRA?

No, but you may be able to roll your 401(k) account over into a traditional IRA. Then, as long as you meet the income requirements (which, remember, get eliminated in 2010), you can convert the traditional IRA to a Roth IRA. Starting in 2008, a provision in the Pension Protection Act allows for direct Roth rollovers.

What are the tax consequences of converting from a traditional IRA to a Roth IRA?

No matter what your age, you will have to pay ordinary income taxes on the money you are transferring in the year that you make the conversion. If you are 70½ or older in the year that you want to convert, be especially aware of IRS rules that prohibit converting any mandatory distributions.

Is a Roth IRA started with conversion money the same as a contributory Roth IRA?

The rules that govern contributory and converted Roth IRAs are identical, with one exception. After you have converted a traditional IRA to a Roth IRA, you'll need to keep the money that was originally converted in the Roth IRA for at least five years or until you are 59½—whichever comes first—before you can withdraw the amount you originally converted. If you withdraw any of the money that was converted from the traditional IRA earlier than that, you will have to pay a penalty on the amount you withdraw. That would, of course, subvert the whole idea of converting to the Roth. Please note that regardless of the amount you originally converted, the earnings on the money you converted will have to stay in the account until you turn 59½ to be withdrawn without penalty. To take the earnings out without penalties *or* taxes, you must be 59½ *and* the account must be more than five years old.

How do I know whether I should convert my traditional IRA to a Roth IRA?

Unless you have a very modest amount of money in your traditional IRA, the money you will owe in taxes may not make it worthwhile to convert to a Roth IRA. In any case, before you make a move, you need to make sure that you will be able to pay for the taxes out of your income or from assets other than your IRA. Keep in mind that you don't have to convert the whole IRA—converting only part of it could minimize your current tax liability. Remember, too, that you have to meet the adjusted gross income requirements for the year in which you are going to convert. In this situation, I'd advise you to consult a professional. Try a certified public account-ant or an enrolled agent (someone legally permitted to do tax returns) who does not make commissions by managing money.

How can I judge if I'm a good candidate to convert my traditional IRA to a Roth IRA?

Here are some general guidelines to help you make your deci-sion:

- Make sure that you have some means of paying the tax bill aside from using your IRA funds. If you don't, converting is not a good idea.
- If the money that you are planning to use to pay the taxes is going to come from the sale of some other investment, will that sale cause you to incur capital-gains or ordinary income taxes? How much future growth will you lose by paying the tax on the conver-sion? Make sure you factor this information into your calculations to see if converting still makes sense.
- Will the additional income from your IRA conversion make your (otherwise nontaxable) Social Security ben-efits taxable or reduce the amount of itemized deduc-tions, personal exemptions, or rental losses during the year of your conversion? Can you afford that? If so, you may want to convert.
- Are you in a relatively low tax bracket right now? Do you expect to be in a higher one by the time that you retire? If both are true, you are a good candidate for conversion.

- Are you close to retirement, and are you planning to use your IRA to live on? If so, it probably doesn't make sense to convert.
- Are you close to retirement but *not* planning to use your IRA money for the foreseeable future? If so, you should consider converting.
- Is your goal to pass your IRA down to your beneficiaries income tax–free? If so, and if you have the money to pay the tax bill now, converting probably makes sense for you.
- Are you concerned that your beneficiaries are goingto have to pay really high income taxes? If so, converting may make sense. Converting can eliminate future income taxation for you and your beneficiaries. Remember, though, that Roth IRAs are included in your gross estate for estate-tax calculations, so your heirs may still need to pay estate tax on your Roth IRA.
- Have you named a charity or some other type of non-profit organization as the beneficiary of your IRA? Since these types of beneficiaries won't have to pay taxes on the bequest anyway, it may not make sense for you to convert. Check with a professional.
- Do you have a nondeductible IRA that hasn't been earning great returns? In this case, converting may make sense, because you have already paid taxes on your contributions and the income from the conversion will only include your earnings, not your contributions. If your nondeductible IRA has been performing well, though, you'll have to run the numbers to see if converting makes sense.

Is there a website that can help me figure out if I should convert to a Roth IRA?

There are actually many websites that can help you do the calculations to answer this question. Just keep in mind that they may have been set up by companies hoping to wind up with your IRA money. I recommend *www.rothira.com,* a site with very good conversion calculators.

Once I have decided to convert from a traditional IRA to a Roth, what is the best way to do it?

The easiest way to convert is to open a Roth IRA account with the same company that has your traditional IRA, assuming they have been doing a satisfactory job for you so far. They can convert the account for you.

What happens if I convert to a Roth IRA and then I find out that I made more than the $100,000 of adjusted gross income that is allowed?

That's no problem; the IRS allows you to transfer the money back to your traditional IRA. This process is known as recharacterization. You should also realize that income qualifications need to be met only for the year you convert.

RECHARACTERIZATION AND RECONVERTING OF A ROTH

What does recharacterization mean?

Recharacterization simply means moving money that was converted to a Roth IRA out of that converted Roth IRA and back into a traditional IRA.

What does reconverting mean?

If you have recharacterized your Roth into a traditional IRA and you want to convert the money back into a Roth again, this transfer is known as a reconversion.

Why would I recharacterize my Roth IRA?

Until 2010, you are allowed to convert a traditional IRA to a Roth only if you meet certain income qualifications. For instance, your modified adjusted gross income or, if you are married, your and your spouse's *combined* modified adjusted gross income must be less than $100,000. Let's say you convert to a Roth IRA, expecting to meet those qualifications, and then you make more money than you anticipated. You no longer meet the conditions to do a Roth conversion, and you must recharacterize it. That is, you must arrange for the assets to go from your Roth back into the traditional IRA.

Is there any reason besides not meeting the income qualifications that I might want to recharacterize my Roth IRA and then later reconvert?

Yes. You might want to recharacterize as a tax strategy. Let's say you convert your traditional IRA to a Roth IRA at the beginning of the year 2007. Over the course of the year, the account loses a significant amount of value. To make matters worse, you are going to be stuck paying taxes on the value of the traditional IRA at the time you converted. If you recharacterize your Roth back to a traditional IRA, you would avoid paying taxes on the amount that you originally converted.

Isn't it worth it to just pay the taxes on the higher value so I can have my money in a converted Roth?

It depends. If you expect to meet the income requirements for a Roth in the next year, it's most likely worth your while to recharacterize and then reconvert back to a Roth.

For example, say you converted a traditional IRA worth $100,000 into a converted Roth IRA in April 2006, and by October it was worth only $50,000. If you leave things as they are, you will owe taxes on that $100,000 conversion. But if you recharacterize your Roth IRA within the allowable time, you will not have to pay taxes for the year 2006 on $100,000. So, let's say it is November 2006 and your account is worth only $50,000. If you recharacterize on November 1, 2006, you will avoid paying taxes on that conversion. Now, let's say that you really want that money in a converted Roth, and as of January 2007, the account is still worth only $50,000. If you now reconvert back to a Roth, you will only be taxed on $50,000, and those taxes won't be due until April 2008. By recharacterizing and then reconverting you have saved paying tax on $50,000—a lot of money by anyone's standards. Make sure that the company holding your converted IRA gives you the option of recharacterizing and reconverting.

How long do I have to recharacterize my Roth?
According to IRS Publication 590, you have until October 15 of the tax year following the year of your original conversion, as long as you file your tax returns in a timely manner.

Last year I recharacterized my Roth IRA, and now I want to reconvert it from a traditional IRA back to a Roth. Are there any time restrictions I need to be aware of?
An IRA owner who converts a traditional IRA to a Roth IRA and then recharacterizes it (that is, changes it back to a traditional IRA) may not reconvert the traditional IRA (change it

to a Roth again) before the beginning of the next tax year or until the end of a 30-day period from the day the Roth IRA was recharacterized, whichever is later.

That sounds complicated, but it's not. An example with dates should clear it up. Let's say that you converted your funds from a traditional IRA to a Roth in the year 2006. You then found out in 2007 that you made too much money to qualify to do a Roth conversion for 2006. You had until October 15, 2007, to do a recharacterization (move the money back into a traditional IRA). On April 15, 2007, you recharacterized your Roth. You cannot reconvert your traditional IRA back to a Roth IRA until May 16, 2007. The IRS stipulates that you must wait until the calendar year after the year of the orginal conversion, or more than 30 days after the date of the recharacterization, whichever date is later, to reconvert—in this case, more than 30 days. However, had you recharacterized on December 20, 2006, you would not be able to reconvert until 30 days after that date, or until about January 19.

IRA ROLLOVER

What is an IRA rollover?

An IRA rollover allows you to transfer (or roll over) assets from your tax-deferred 401(k) to another tax-deferred investment vehicle. Because both investments are tax-deferred, there is no tax consequence when you make the transfer. When you ultimately withdraw the funds, usually at age 59½ or older, the money will be taxed as ordinary income in the year of withdrawal.

How long do I have to transfer my money from a 401(k) plan to an IRA rollover?

If you take possession of your 401(k) funds yourself, you have 60 days from the date of receipt to get them into your rollover account. If you miss the deadline, you will be taxed on the entire withdrawal, and if you are not at least 59½, you also will be hit with a 10 percent penalty.

But the transfer of such funds is usually done from custodian to custodian. You open up an IRA rollover account at a brokerage firm (my preference), a bank, an insurance company, or a mutual-fund company, and it arranges the transfer from your 401(k) into the new account. This is the best way to do a rollover, since the custodian of your 401(k) plan will not be required temporarily to withhold 20 percent of the money for possible taxes.

What are the advantages of an IRA rollover?

One advantage is that most IRA rollovers give you an unlimited choice of mutual funds, stocks, and bonds in which to invest your money, and you can usually trade as often and as many times as you want to. You can usually place orders to buy or sell by phone, and your transactions are usually confirmed immediately. You also may have access to a professional financial adviser.

Are there any disadvantages to an IRA rollover?

If you use a full-service broker, you will probably be charged annual fees and commissions. If you are younger than 59½, you can withdraw your IRA money only through substantially equal periodic payments (SEPP) or annuitization to avoid the 10 percent early-withdrawal penalty—unless you meet one of the exceptions for medical expenses, etc. You must begin to make withdrawals from your IRA by April 1 of the year after you turn 70½. Also, personal creditors may be able to reach your IRA account, whereas, under ERISA rules, they can't touch your 401(k) or 403(b).

If I'm younger than 55 in the year I retire, is an IRA rollover the way to go?

Possibly. The flexibility and greater number of investment options could make this a better choice than a company plan. If you have a really large amount of money in your plan and you are going to seek professional financial advice, you might want to consider dividing your rollover between two advisers to see which one performs better.

If I'm older than 55, which makes more sense?

If you are between the ages of 55 and 59½ in the year you retire, leave at least some of your money in the company plan (as long as you are allowed to). That way, you can take advantage of the investment flexibility of an IRA and you'll also have access to the money in your 401(k) without that 10 percent penalty limitation of an IRA.

If you are over age 59½ in the year you retire, the decision is up to you. If you qualify for ten-year averaging and you want to leave that possibility open, leave the money in your company's plan. If you want to expand your investment opportunities, an IRA rollover gives you the opportunity to do so.

RETIREMENT PLANS FOR THE SELF-EMPLOYED

If you're self-employed and are not an incorporated entity, you, too, have excellent options for funding your (and your employees') retirement. You can open what is known as a sim-plified employee pension (SEP) plan, a Keogh, or a SIMPLE. All three of these are tax-deferred pension plans, and great ways to save for retirement. In order to qualify for these accounts, your earnings must be reported on Form 1099-MISC, or earned as fees for services you've provided. If people work for you, you'll have to fund SEP, Keogh, or SIMPLE plans for them as well. Most retirement accounts for theself-employed are governed by the same restrictions as IRAand 401(k) plans. You should consult a professional for exact guidelines in your situation, but, in general, the same 10 per-cent penalty for withdrawing money before the age of 59½ applies; all money withdrawn will be taxed as ordinary income in the year of withdrawal, unless you and your plan qualify for ten-year averaging; and in most cases you have to start taking money out by April 1 of the year you turn 70½.

What is a SEP-IRA?

SEP plan stands for simplified employee pension plan. It's essentially an extended IRA for self-employed people and their employees. But whereas in an IRA you can contribute a maximum in 2006–2007 of only $4,000 a year (increasing in following years; please see page 111), in a SEP-IRA you can contribute up to $45,000 to your own account in 2007 (the latest year available as of this writing), or 25 percent of your net income, as income is defined for these purposes by IRS, whichever is less; and up to $45,000 per year per employee, or 25 percent of his or her salary, whichever is less.

Where can I set up a SEP-IRA?

SEP-IRAs can be established virtually anywhere you would like to invest—at a bank, a mutual-fund company, or a bro-kerage firm.

For an employer, what is the downside of a SEP-IRA?

If you fund a SEP for yourself and have employees who have worked for you for three of the past five years, you are also required to fund their SEPs (as of 2007, up to a maximum of either $45,000 or 25 percent of their salary, whichever is less). The money in these accounts vests automatically, and if your employees leave tomorrow, they will be able to take that money with them. With a SEP-IRA, employees are 100 percent vested at all times.

Can I have a SEP-IRA and a Roth IRA?

Yes. You can have both a Roth IRA and a SEP if you meet the income requirements.

Is it possible to convert a SEP-IRA to a Roth IRA?

Yes. This particular conversion can make a lot of sense, because it allows you to invest more than the maximum allowed per year in a Roth. Let's say that your income would allow you to contribute $12,400 a year to a SEP-IRA. You can make that deposit and then, as long as your total income is less than $100,000 that year, you can convert that SEP-IRA to a Roth. (The $100,000 income limit gets eliminated in 2010.) Essentially, you will have managed to put a great deal more than the annual limit into a Roth. You will have to pay taxes on the $12,400 after you convert, but you can deduct that same $12,400 from your income as a SEP-IRA deduction. If you are self-employed, consult a tax specialist to see how much you could contribute to a SEP-IRA, and consider making this conversion.

What is a Keogh plan?

A Keogh is a somewhat more complicated plan than a SEP-IRA, but it may allow you to save more money. The added benefit carries with it more immediate responsibility to your employees. If you fund a Keogh for yourself, you must also fund a Keogh for any employee who has worked for you for more than one year (two years if there is full vesting required in no more than two years).

There are three types of Keogh plans. The two most common types are a money-purchase plan and a profit-sharing plan. In both, you can put aside up to 25 percent of your qualified net income, as defined by the IRS (up to a maximum of $45,000 in 2007, the latest year available as of this writing), and invest the money in any way you choose. But be careful: In a money-purchase plan, when you open the account, you establish the percentage of your own (and of any employees') net earnings that you must continue to contribute each year from that time on, and that percentage cannot be changed. It doesn't matter whether you have a great year financially or a terrible one, you must still contribute the same percentage of your own (and of any employees') income to the money-purchase Keogh. Profit-sharing Keoghs are more flexible, in that you have discretion as to how much or how little to contribute each year, up to the maximum amounts allowed by the IRS.

The third type of plan, a defined-benefit plan, may allow much larger contributions for you and your employees. However, contributions are required every year, whether or not there are profits, in the amount determined by an actuary to be necessary to reach a defined benefit.

It is possible to create a combination of Keogh plans to give you the maximum opportunity to save while maintaining some flexibility. Consult your tax adviser.

If I need money, can I borrow from my Keogh plan?

It depends. If you have a Keogh and you own more than 10 percent of your business, then the answer is no. Heed this rule—for if you do borrow, you will be subject to a 15 percent penalty yearly for any outstanding loan amount. If, however, you own less than 10 percent of the business, you are free to take a loan from your Keogh plan.

What if I took out a loan from my Keogh two years ago and I do own more than 10 percent of the business?

Well, you're in trouble. You are required to file Form 5330 and to repay the loan and pay the penalty within seven months of the end of the year in which you took out the loan. Since you did not, the penalty will now be 100 percent.

SIMPLE IRA

What is a SIMPLE IRA?

A Savings Incentive Match Plan for Employees (SIMPLE) is an IRA set up by a small employer for the company's employees. Employees may contribute a percentage of their salary, up to $10,500 (or $13,000 if you are 50 or older) in the year 2007, to their SIMPLE IRA and will receive some level of a matching percentage from their employer. (The maximum contribution in subsequent years will be indexed to inflation.) The employer must match contributions according to a certain formula. The employer and the employee together may contribute up to $15,000 in the year 2007 to the participant's account.

Do I have to set up a SIMPLE plan for all my employees?

No. Only employees who made at least $5,000 in any two prior years and are projected to earn at least $5,000 during the current year are eligible for SIMPLE IRAs.

How much of my employees' contributions am I required to match?

As a self-employed person with eligible employees, you either will have to follow a matching-contribution formula or a 2 percent contribution formula. If you choose the matching formula, you must match the dollar amount each employee contributes to the plan, up to a range of 1 to 3 percent of his or her salary. (You can choose a 1 percent match for up to two of any five years.) Under the 2 percent contribution formula, you, the employer, agree to contribute 2 percent of the employee's salary up to a maximum of $4,500 per year (for the year 2007) for each employee, regardless of whether the employee makes any contribution that year. All these contributions, by the way, are vested the moment they are made, which means that any contributing employee can withdraw them if he or she leaves your company. Between your contribution for your employee and what he deposits for himself, in the year 2007 an employee may have up to $15,000 a year invested in a SIMPLE.

Can I have a SIMPLE IRA and a Roth IRA?

Yes, as long as you meet the income qualifications of a Roth.

I work for myself. What retirement plan do I want: a SEP, a Keogh, or a SIMPLE?

If paperwork makes you crazy, you should know that there's more paperwork involved with a Keogh than with a SEP or a SIMPLE (the paperwork requirements for which are almost nil). Once you have more than $100,000 in a Keogh account, and only you and your spouse or you and your business partners and spouses are covered, you'll have to file a 5500EZ form—it's not all that bad, but it's still paperwork, and paperwork is not required with a SEP or a SIMPLE. If the maximum contribution to a SEP or a SIMPLE meets your needs, you're better off staying away from the Keogh. If your income warrants it and you can use that extra tax break, then a Keogh is the way to go.

If you're self-employed, you should definitely take advantage of one of these options. Just don't forget that employees are 100 percent vested at all times with a SIMPLE IRA or a SEP-IRA. With a Keogh, there is a vesting schedule. Check with a professional.

If I take money out of a SIMPLE the year after I open it, will I have to pay a 10 percent early-withdrawal penalty if I'm younger than 59½?

It's worse than that—if you take money out of your SIMPLE plan within the first two years of opening it, your early-withdrawal penalty won't be 10 percent—it will be 25 percent. After the first two years, the penalty drops to 10 percent.

RETIREMENT TAX CREDIT

What is the retirement tax credit?

The retirement tax credit—which Congress made permanent in 2006—was part of the Economic Growth and Tax Relief Reconciliation Act of 2001. If you meet the eligibility requirements, the retirement tax credit is free money, so make sure you don't miss out. As of 2007, single filers with income under $26,000 and head-of-household filers with income below $39,000 can get a credit of as much as 50 percent of the amount invested in a retirement account, up to a $1,000 credit on a $4,000 contribution. That's $1,000 off your tax bill. It's like the IRS paid for a quarter of your retirement.

Put $4,000 in an IRA. If you're in the 27 percent bracket, that saves you $1,080. You also get the $1,000 credit. That means that you're only out of pocket $1,920 on a $4,000 investment.

This credit is available for elective contributions to a 401(k) plan, 403(b) annuity, SIMPLE, or SEP. It also covers contributions to a traditional or Roth IRA and voluntary after-tax employee-qualified plans. You must also be at least age 18, not a full-time student, and not claimed as a dependent on another person's return.

The credit is based on adjusted gross income as follows:

JOINT FILERS	HEAD OF HOUSEHOLD	SINGLE	CREDIT RATE
$0–$31,000	$0–$23,250	$0–$15,500	50%
$31,001–$34,000	$23,251–$25,500	$15,501–$17,000	20%
$34,001–$52,000	$25,501–$39,000	$17,001–$26,000	10%
Over $52,000	Over $39,000	Over $26,000	0%

TAXATION OF RETIREMENT-PLAN WITHDRAWALS

How are the funds I withdraw from my retirement account taxed?

Apart from withdrawals from a Roth IRA (which, if done correctly, are tax-free), most withdrawals from retirement plans are taxed as ordinary income. There is one exception. If you meet certain restrictions, money withdrawn from a qualified retirement plan using the technique known as ten-year averaging is taxed differently.

TEN-YEAR AVERAGING

What is ten-year averaging? Who is eligible for it?

If you were born before January 1, 1936, you may be able to take advantage of a favorable tax treatment known as ten-year averaging. Here's how it works: First, you are required to withdraw your retirement-plan money in one lump sum. You figure out how much you owe in taxes by dividing the total value of your account by 10, then adding $2,480 to that figure. Look up the 1986 single taxpayer rate for that amount, then take that number and multiply it by 10: That is how much you would owe on the total withdrawal. For an amount under $400,000, ten-year averaging could save you a considerable sum.

But there are restrictions. To be eligible to use ten-year averaging:

- You must have been born before January 1, 1936.
- You must withdraw all the money in your qualified retirement plan in a lump sum.
- You cannot roll over some of your money and apply ten-year averaging to the rest.
- You must have participated in your retirement plan for at least five years.

Please note: You can apply ten-year averaging only once in a lifetime.

If I qualify for ten-year averaging, should I do it?

It depends on how much your retirement plan's distributions would be, and also whether you need the money from your account right away or can afford to let it sit for a while, either in the plan or in an IRA rollover. If you have a few hundred thousand dollars in your plan, for example, it is not worth it to give up the use of the money that you will use to pay the taxes when it could be accumulating value for many years.

Besides ten-year averaging, is there any other way to get money out of a qualified retirement plan and not have to pay ordinary income taxes?

Yes, there are two. First, the tax law provides a special benefit if your company retirement plan includes stock of your company and that stock has appreciated in value within the plan. If you take a lump-sum withdrawal of the assets in your company plan, you will be taxed on your company stock in the plan based on the cost to the plan of the stock rather than on its value at the time of distribution. In addition, if you hold your stock for longer than a year, when you sell it you will get long-term capital-gains treatment for the difference between the cost of the stock to the plan and the stock's value at the time of the distribution. This difference is known as the net unrealized appreciation.

Second, you can pay capital-gains tax on your withdrawal. If you were born before January 1, 1936, *and* you have been in your qualified plan since before 1974, you can treat some of your distributions as capital gains, subject only to a flat 10 percent tax rate. The administrator of your plan will let you know if any amount of your retirement account is eligible for capital-gains treatment. Even if you are eligible, you should consult with a tax professional before making a withdrawal.

MANDATORY WITHDRAWAL FROM A RETIREMENT ACCOUNT

When do I have to start taking money out of my retirement account(s)?

You are required to begin withdrawing money from a traditional IRA and a 401(k) (or a Keogh, SEP, or SIMPLE) by April 1 of the year after you turn 70½. With respect to a 401(k)—but not a traditional IRA—if you are still working at age 70½ for the company that holds your plan, this mandatory withdrawal rule does not apply, provided you do not own more than 5 percent of the company you work for. In that case, you will not have to begin making withdrawals until April 1 of the year after the year you retire. Please note that with a Roth IRA, these mandatory withdrawal rules do not apply; you can leave your money in a Roth IRA for as long as you like, even until your death.

Once I turn 70½ and I need to start making IRA withdrawals, how do I know how much I should take?

The custodian of your IRA should help you determine the exact figure. The custodian's calculations are based on how much money you have in all of your IRAs and on the new Uniform Distribution Table. (Every taxpayer now uses this table, regardless of the named beneficiary—unless the sole beneficiary is the spouse *and* the spouse is more than ten years younger than the account holder. In that case, taxpayers will use the table for the actual joint life expectancy of the taxpayer and spouse, which will result in a lower required distribution than the Uniform Distribution Table.)

To determine how much you should withdraw, simply take the total value of your account and divide it by the appropriate figure on the table—that is how much you will be expected to withdraw in the first year after you turn 70½. People with IRAs often find it difficult to understand what decisions have to be made when they reach age 70½. One of the most helpful publications on this topic is *Barry Picker's Guide to Retirement Distribution Planning,* which can be ordered online at *www.BPickerCPA.com* or by calling (800) 809-0015. I recommend it highly.

Can I change my beneficiary after I have started taking withdrawals from my IRA?

Yes, you can. This is one of the great advantages of the new regulations. You can now change your beneficiary at any time, and the change will not affect your lifetime distributions.

Is it smart to postpone taking money out of my IRA until April 1 of the year after I turn 70½?

It depends on your tax bracket. In most cases, it's not wise to postpone your first withdrawal, since you'll have to take two distributions in the same year—one distribution for the year that you were 70½, and the other for the present year. By postponing your IRA withdrawal that first year, you could find yourself in a higher tax bracket the second year as a result of taking two years' worth of withdrawals in one tax year.

BENEFICIARY WITHDRAWALS

The rules for beneficiary withdrawals after the death of the account holder are pretty much the same for all retirement accounts, including IRAs, 401(k)s, 403(b)s, etc. Please note that the following answers apply to both contributory Roth IRAs and Roth IRA conversions.

What happens to the money in my retirement plan when I die?

When you die, your money goes to the beneficiaries you named on your retirement plan application forms. (Even if your will or trust dictates that all your money is to go to your brother, your primary beneficiary on your application is the person who will get the money in your retirement account[s].) What your beneficiary can do with the money depends on whether he or she is your surviving spouse and what is in your retirement plan document. The laws on what happens to a retirement account (or accounts) when a surviving spouse is the beneficiary are very different from those on what happens when the beneficiary is not the spouse.

If I survive my spouse and I am the beneficiary, what can I do with the retirement account?

As the surviving spouse, your options depend on whether or not your spouse had started taking the minimum required distributions.

What are my options if my deceased spouse had already started withdrawing money?

If your spouse had already started taking the required minimum distribution before he or she died, you can do one of three things, provided the plan permits them:

1. Continue taking the distributions, which will now be based on your life expectancy, recalculated each year. If you die before emptying the account, the remaining

balance at your death will be distributed to your heirs over the remaining years in your life expectancy. Your remaining life expectancy will not be recalculated.

2. Accelerate the distributions—that is, take them more frequently.

3. Stop the distributions and transfer the account to a retirement account in your own name. Then start taking the distributions by either April 1 of the year after you turn 70½, or December 31 of the year after the year of your spouse's death, whichever comes later.

What should I do if my deceased spouse hadn't started to take distributions?

If your spouse had not started taking the required minimum distributions, you have many more choices:

1. You can roll the account over into your own retirement account and treat it as if it were your money— which is exactly what it now is. This means you can continue to make contributions to the IRA or roll other money that you may have from a company retirement plan into it. In my opinion, this is usually the best option, especially if your late spouse was older than you. If not, please see No. 5 in this list.

2. In the case of an IRA and other retirement accounts that permit it, you can keep the account just as it is, in your deceased spouse's name. However, if you do this, you must start taking money out of the IRA either by December 31 of the year your spouse would have turned 70½, or December 31 of the year after your spouse died, whichever is later. I would be hard-pressed to think of a reason to do this with the money, unless your situation falls into that described in No. 5.

3. You can withdraw the money in a lump sum. I don't endorse this option; the taxes could be substantial.

4. If you keep a retirement account in your deceased spouse's name, you can make withdrawals from it over the next five years, or make periodic withdrawals over your life expectancy. If you want to use the "five-year rule," you would need to inform the IRS of your intention to do so. But I can't think of any way that you would benefit from this.

5. If you keep a retirement account in your deceased spouse's name, you do not have to take any money until the end of the year when your deceased spouse would have turned 70½. You might do this if your deceased spouse was much younger than you, and you want to continue to defer income taxes on the money for as long as possible. You might also want to do this if you are younger than 59½ and need to make more withdrawals. If you roll the IRA into your own name and withdraw money before you're 59½, you may be subject to the 10 percent early-withdrawal penalty.

Most people roll their late spouses' accounts over into an IRA in their own name; it gives them the greatest number of options.

What are my choices if someone other than my spouse leaves me a retirement plan account?

If someone other than your spouse leaves you a retirement account, you should be able to take minimum distributions based on your own life expectancy, provided the plan permits it. You can always just take the money out in a lump sum, but you might have quite a tax bill on your hands.

If the owner of the account had not started taking minimum distributions, then you have two choices, with one variation:

- By December 31 of the fifth year after the IRA owner's death, the entire account must be emptied. You must withdraw all the money from the account by that date. I can't think of any reason why you would do this.
- You can take out a minimum amount of money each year, calculated on your life expectancy. This is clearly the better option, and this option is now the default under new IRS regulations.

Of course, you can always take out more anytime you want. The above choices are simply the best options available if you want to take the least amount out.

After I die, will beneficiaries other than my spouse owe income tax on the assets I leave to them in my Roth IRA?

Not as long as the five-year holding period has passed. If the five-year period is up, your beneficiaries can withdraw all the money from a Roth immediately, with no income-tax implications whatsoever. If five years have not yet passed, your beneficiaries need to be cautious. If they withdraw more than the amount you originally contributed or converted to a Roth, they will owe ordinary income taxes on the earnings.

What if the five-year holding period has not passed?

If your beneficiaries take distributions over their own life expectancies, starting no later than December 31 of the year following the year in which you die, then they probably will not be withdrawing earnings until the five-year period has passed.

If my beneficiary is not 59½, will he or she have to pay the 10 percent penalty upon withdrawal?

No. The 10 percent early-withdrawal penalty never applies to beneficiaries' withdrawals of money in a Roth IRA, regardless of age or how long the money has been in the account.

If my beneficiary is my wife and I leave my Roth IRA to her, when does she have to take the money out of the account?

Your wife does not have to do anything with that money. She can treat the Roth IRA as her own. She can let it grow, withdraw it gradually, or take a lump-sum payment—the choice is hers.

STOCK OPTIONS AND STOCK-PURCHASE PLANS

What kinds of employee stock options are available as part of a retirement package?

There are two kinds of stock-option plans available to employees: nonqualified stock-option plans (NQSOs) and incentive stock-option plans (ISOs). Both types of plans give employees of a particular company the opportunity (or option) to purchase a particular amount of the company's stock for a fixed price within a specified period. Acting on this opportunity is known as exercising the option, and the fixed price is known as the exercise price.

What are the main differences between nonqualified stock-option plans and incentive stock-option plans?

The two main differences between nonqualified stock-option plans and incentive stock-option plans are how they are taxed and who is eligible to receive the options.

With an NQSO, you are subject to ordinary income taxes and withholding for Social Security and Medicare as soon as you exercise those options.

With an ISO, you are not subject to these taxes when you exercise your option. However, when you exercise an ISO, you are subject to the alternative minimum tax (AMT), an income tax calculated by a different set of rules than those used to calculate regular income tax.

You cannot be given an ISO if you are not an employee of the company that is offering the options; outside consultants, for instance, cannot receive ISOs. An NQSO can be granted to consultants, as well as to employees of a corporation.

How do nonqualified stock-option plans work?

Let's say your employer offers you a nonqualified stock option to purchase up to 200 shares of the company stock during the next ten years, and the exercise price for that stock is $10 per share. That means that you can exercise your option, or purchase up to 200 shares of stock at $10 per share, at any time over the next ten years, regardless of the value of that stock. Say you waited to purchase your stock, and the price of the stock shot up to $100 per share. It is your right to exercise your stock options at $10 a share. But when you do this, you will be taxed on the difference between your exercise price of $10 and the value of the stock at the time you exercised the option ($100). In this example, you would owe ordinary income taxes on $90 per share for every share that you exercised. The $90 per share is called the *bargain element,* or spread.

When I exercise an NQSO, do I owe capital-gains tax at the rate of 20 percent? Or do I have to pay ordinary income tax on the spread?

Because you didn't actually own the stock until you exercised the option, this money isn't considered capital gains. You will pay ordinary income tax.

When is the tax due?

You will be subject to income tax, Social Security, and Medicare withholding taxes right away, even if you only exercise the option and do not sell the underlying stock. Make sure you have the money to pay for the taxes as well as the money for the exercise price at the time you exercise.

I exercised some options but was not allowed to sell the stock right away. I was also told that I didn't owe taxes yet. Why?

You probably were in what is known as a "blackout period." During a blackout period, the Securities and Exchange Commission prohibits anyone from selling the underlying stock. The SEC imposes blackout periods to prevent people who hold too many stock options from diluting the market for that stock or profiting too soon from stock movements. Blackout periods also affect your taxes. Federal taxes are not due until the blackout period is over. If you exercise your options during a blackout period, you must make a tax decision that cannot be reversed: You must choose whether to report to the IRS the price of the stock at the date of exercise or the price when the blackout period ends.

When the blackout period is over, will I still owe taxes only on the difference between the exercise price and the share price on the day I exercised the options?

It depends. You can elect to recognize that taxable income on the date that you exercise your options, or you can postpone the income taxes until the blackout period is over. If you postpone, you will owe ordinary income taxes on the difference between the exercise price and the price of the stock on the day that the blackout period ends, not on the day you exercised your options. If you choose to pay the taxes on the day you exercise the option, even though you are in a blackout period, you can file an election under IRC section 83(b). Remember that you have only 30 days from the time the stock is transferred to you to file this election. Please check with your tax adviser to see if it makes sense for you to postpone the taxes in this situation or to pay them up front.

EXERCISE TIME

I plan to exercise my NQSOs and hold on to my stock for more than a year. That way, when I sell the stock, all I have to pay on my gains is long-term capital-gains tax. Is this wise?

Exercising your options early might seem to be a good tax strategy, but in almost all circumstances you are actually better off if you don't. For you to benefit from exercising early, the stock must go up in value considerably after you've exercised your options. How far up? The rule of thumb is at least 16 percent. If the stock price does not go up by at least that much, exercising early really isn't worth it. Remember, when you exercise an NQSO, you not only have to come up with the money to exercise the option, you also have to come up with the money to pay the taxes due (please see the previous question). In most cases, exercising your options and holding on to the stock doesn't enhance your return, regardless of the tax benefits.

Can exercising my options early work against me?

Yes. Let's say you decide to exercise 5,000 shares of NQSOs, and the exercise price is $5 a share. To buy the stock, you will have to come up with $25,000 (5,000 shares × $5) in cash. Let's say the stock is trading on the market for $100 a share. You're happy—you now have $500,000 worth of stock. But the downside is that you owe income taxes on $475,000—the difference between your exercise price and the market price of the stock. After you exercise your options, if you hold the stock for at least 12 months and a day before selling it, you will owe only capital-gains tax on the difference between the $100 per share and whatever it is worth when you sell it. In this scenario, if the stock is trading at $150 a share when you finally sell it, you will owe capital gains tax on $250,000 (5,000 shares × $50), but don't forget that you have already paid ordinary income tax on that first $95 per share. Plus you will have lost the use of $25,000 the year you exercised the options, not to mention the income tax on that $475,000, which would be about $200,000. All this just so you could pay a lower tax rate on the increase of the stock price a year down the road. That's a big gamble. What if the price of the stock goes down? Too bad. You still will have to pay the tax due when you exercise the options.

This also holds true for ISOs, especially if your marginal income-tax bracket is 28 percent or lower. If you are in a higher tax bracket, check with your tax adviser to see if exercising your options early makes sense for you. Please remember, the more volatile your stock (how much and how frequently it fluctuates in relation to the market), the more risk you take in exercising and holding the stock. Most people are better off if they exercise and sell at the same time.

CASHLESS TRANSACTIONS

My company is offering a cashless transaction when I want to exercise my options. How does that work?

Many employees exercise their options when they need to make a down payment on a major purchase, such as a home or a new car. Let's say your underlying stock is selling at $150 a share, and you want to exercise 1,000 options at an exercise price of $50 a share. This means you have to come up with $50,000 in cash to exercise those options. What if you do not have that $50,000? It stands to reason that if somebody needs to sell stock to make a down payment, that employee probably doesn't have the cash needed to exercise the options in the first place. This is where the cashless transaction comes in (although "cashless" may be a misnomer, as it could cost you in the end). Your company has probably made an arrangement with a brokerage firm whereby when you exercise your option, the brokerage firm will sell the underlying stock on the very same day. In essence, you have been able to exercise your options without having to come up with any cash. Three business days later, you will get the difference between your exercise price and the price for which the brokerage firm sold the stock, minus any fees the company takes for allowing you to do this.

If your company doesn't, pay your friendly banker a visit. Since you have the options, the bank may use them as collateral and make you a short-term loan for the amount you need to exercise the options. Once the stock is sold, you repay the bank the principal it loaned you plus setup fees and interest. These fees and interest will be far less than that 25 percent your company could charge you.

INCENTIVE STOCK OPTIONS

How are incentive stock options taxed when exercised?
When you exercise an ISO, you may be subject to the alternative minimum tax (AMT) amount. When the options are exercised, the AMT is calculated on the difference between market value and the exercise price. Because the AMT is calculated differently than regular income tax, please consult a tax professional.

With incentive stock options, you pay income tax only when you sell the stock. How long you hold the stock will determine whether you pay ordinary income tax or capital-gains tax. After exercising your options, if you hold the stock for more than a year before selling it, you will pay capital-gains tax, assuming that was more than two years from the date the option was granted. If you hold your stock for a year or less, you will pay ordinary income tax.

What happens if I don't hold the stock for more than one year before selling it?
Such a sale is called a disqualified disposition, and the option spread (the value of the stock when you exercised the option less the option price, or the sale price less the option price, whichever is higher) is taxed at your ordinary income-tax rate, not at the capital-gains tax rate. Any gain beyond the option spread is taxed as capital gains.

I am eligible to exercise ISOs worth about $125,000. Does the value of the options have any bearing on the tax treatment?
Yes. Any stock options worth more than $100,000 that first become eligible to be exercised in one calendar year are automatically converted to NQSOs.

Are there any time constraints on when I can exercise my ISOs?

Yes. Usually you must exercise your options within ten years from the time they were granted to you. If you happen to own more than 10 percent of all the classes of stock of a corporation (or of corporations that are directly related to that stock), you must exercise your options within five years.

Do I have to exercise the options? What if the stock is selling at a lower price than the exercise price?

You don't have to exercise options if you don't want to. But if the specified time period passes and the options expire, your options will not be renewed.

Can I still exercise my stock options once I am retired?

This is a question many people forget to ask when they prepare to retire. Most ISOs can be exercised only while you are an employee of the corporation that granted the options—or within a specified time of leaving that corporation. It is not uncommon for a company either to terminate an employee's right to exercise stock options or to reduce the amount of time an employee has to purchase stock after retirement. So if you retire in year six of a ten-year stock option, you might not be able to carry that option with you for another four years. If you have options that you want to exercise, either purchase the stock before you retire or be certain that you have the option to do so after you leave the company.

I am leaving my place of employment because I sustained a disability. Do I have to exercise my ISOs within three months of leaving?

Maybe not. If you are considered disabled according to the

Internal Revenue Service's definition, you have an extended period, up to 12 months, in which to exercise your ISOs.

How do I make sure that I can exercise my stock options?

Read your stock-option agreement with care, paying particularly close attention to the exercise dates. If there is anything that you do not understand, consult both your company's human resources department and a financial planning professional immediately.

Can I transfer my ISO to someone else?

No. ISOs are not transferable, though they can be inherited.

If I should die, can my spouse or life partner exercise my options?

Read the option agreement that granted you the options to begin with. Don't be surprised if your options must be exercised within three months to a year after your death by the personal representative of the estate—in other words, by a court-appointed executor. The problem starts here, for it could take more than three months to get that person appointed by the court. What I suggest you do is establish a revocable living trust and in the powers section of that trust give the trustee the right to exercise your options after your death. That way, your heirs have a better chance of not needing to appoint a representative.

STOCK WARRANTS

In 2003 Microsoft stopped issuing stock options and started issuing warrants. Can you tell me the difference between stock options and stock warrants?

Both a stock warrant and a stock option grant the holders the ability to exercise the warrant/option before an expiration date, for a certain number of shares at a specified price. The stock warrant allows the holder to buy stock at a fixed price, with the ability to sell at a far higher price, and thus make a profit. If the price of the security rises above the warrant's exercise price, then the holder can buy the security at the warrant's exercise price and resell it for a profit. Otherwise, the warrant will simply expire or remain unused. Warrants are traded on option exchanges as securities whose price reflects the value of the underlying stock. With a stock option, employees do not acquire the stock until they "exercise" the options, and usually the employee sells the stock immediately to cash in on any rise in value above the price he or she paid for it. The potential loss of a stock option is limited to the price paid to acquire the option. When an option is not exercised, it expires. No shares change hands, and the money spent to purchase the option is lost. A stock option is issued by independent parties, such as a member of the Chicago Board Options Exchange, while a stock warrant is issued and guaranteed by the corporation that issued the common stock. The lifetime of a warrant is often years, while the lifetime of an option is generally months.

STOCK-PURCHASE PLAN

My company offers a stock-purchase plan as a retirement-planning strategy. What is this?

Typically, with a stock-purchase plan, employees can designate an amount of money to be withheld from their regular paychecks and used to buy stock in the company, sometimes at rates discounted from the market price. The money then grows (or shrinks!) tax-deferred until the employee sells the stock, usually after an extended period. While it's fine to take advantage of a tax-deferred growth opportunity, it's important to remain diversified in your stock holdings—you are already very dependent on your employer for a paycheck, so you don't want to have all your retirement savings riding on the company's fortunes as well.

VESTED VS. NONVESTED STOCK

What is the difference between vested stock and non-vested stock?
Your stock is considered vested if, according to the agreement you made with your employer, you retain the full value of the stock no matter what happens. "No matter what happens" includes your quitting your job or getting fired. It also means that you have the right, if you wish, to transfer this stock to anyone you want. Any agreement other than this means that you have been given nonvested stock.

Does nonvested stock stay that way? Or can my stock become vested over time?
Your stock may become vested over time.

What are the tax rules of being given stock as compensation?
It depends on whether you were given vested or nonvested stock. If your stock is fully vested when you receive it, its value (minus the amount paid for it, if any) will be taxed as ordinary income. If the stock is not vested, it cannot be taxed until it vests. If you get nonvested stock, however, you have 30 days to make a section 83(b) election. Under this provision, the value of the stock is reported as income when you acquired it (and when its share price was likely lower), instead of the year it

vests. The tax consequences are based on the fair market value of the stock.

Can the company force me to sell the stock back to them if I lose my job?

In many cases, it can. It all depends on the terms of your agreement. If you paid for this stock when you acquired it, you may have agreed to sell it back at the same amount you paid for it, or at its fair market value.

What is the fair market value of a stock? How does the IRS figure this out?

The classical definition of fair market value is this: the price at which the property would change hands between a willing buyer and a willing seller, neither being under any compulsion to buy or to sell, and both having reasonable knowledge of relevant facts.

PENSION PLANS: KNOWING YOUR RIGHTS

I've heard stories about companies mismanaging pension plans, leaving their employees with nothing, and that makes me nervous. How can I keep track of what my company does with my retirement plan?

The Employee Retirement Income Security Act of 1974 (ERISA) is a federal law that sets minimum standards for pension plans in private industry. ERISA requires retirement plan administrators—the people who run the plans—to provide you with written information explaining the most important facts about your pension plan. The plan administrator is required to keep you regularly informed. This includes a summary plan description (SPD), which you should get when you begin participating in the plan. The SPD is a comprehensive document that tells you exactly what the plan provides and how it operates. The SPD should show when you began to participate in the plan, how your service and benefits are calculated, when your benefit becomes vested, when and how you will receive payments, and how to file for your benefits when you need to. If there are any changes to the SPD, your plan administrator is required to give you a revised summary plan description or a separate document detailing the modifications. Both the original SPD and any changes to it must be given to you free, and you should read everything carefully.

In addition to the SPD, the plan administrator must give you a copy of the plan's summary annual report, a summary of the yearly financial report that most pension plans must file with the Department of Labor. Finally, you should also receive, free of charge every year, an individual benefit statement that describes your personal total accrued and vested benefits.

If this information does not answer the questions you have about your plan, there is more information available, but you must request it from your plan administrator.

I haven't been able to get the summary plan description, the summary annual report, or the annual report from my plan administrator. How do I figure out what is going on?

If no one else you know in your plan is receiving this information either, this is potentially a serious case of mismanagement. Because the annual report has to be filed with the government, you may be able to obtain a copy of it by writing to the Department of Labor, EBSA, Public Disclosure Room, Room

N-5638, 200 Constitution Avenue NW, Washington, D.C. 20210 *www.dol.gov/ebsa*. When you make a request, try to provide as much information as possible about the plan. The Department of Labor will charge you a modest fee to cover copying costs.

Meanwhile, make sure that you have made your requests to your plan administrator in writing and have kept copies of the requests. If a plan administrator refuses to comply with your request for documents, and the reasons for the delay were within his or her control, a court could impose penalties on the administrator of up to $100 per day.

Is it possible for my retirement plan to be terminated? What would that mean for my retirement savings?

Pension plans are supposed to continue indefinitely, but employers are allowed to terminate plans. You do have some protection if your plan is canceled. If your plan is a qualified plan, your accrued benefit must become 100 percent vested when the plan terminates, to the extent that it is funded—meaning what has so far been contributed by you and your employer. This is also true if your employer partially terminates a qualified plan, for example, if one division of a company is closed and a substantial number of plan participants are affected. All affected employees' plans become 100 percent vested, to the extent they have been funded, effective as soon as the plan terminates.

When my sister's pension plan was terminated, the company she works for didn't have enough money to pay out all the benefits. How can I make sure this doesn't happen to me?

If you have a defined-benefit plan, ask your plan administrator if it is insured by the Pension Benefit Guaranty Corporation

(PBGC). If it is, the PBGC guarantees that you will receive your vested pension benefits, up to certain limits. If additional benefits that exceed the PBGC's limits or that were not guaranteed are due to you, whether you receive them and how much you receive will depend on the plan's funding and how much the PBGC can recover from your employer. If you find yourself in this messy situation, contact the Pension Benefit Guaranty Corporation, Administrative Review and Technical Assistance Department, 1200 K Street NW, Washington, D.C. 20005, (202) 326-4000 (*www.pbgc.gov*) for more information.

Rumors of a possible merger are flying around my office. Should I be worried about my pension plan?

If your employer merges with another company, the two companies may merge retirement plans as well. But if your company's plan is the one that gets terminated, you would most likely receive benefits under the new plan that are at least equal to the benefits you were entitled to before the plans merged. By all means, ask your plan administrator what's going on.

What if I lose my job but I am vested in my pension? Will I keep receiving information about my pension?

If you leave an employer with whom you have a vested pension benefit that you won't be eligible to receive until later in life, your plan administrator must report that information to you and to the IRS, which, in turn, will inform the Social Security Administration. You can check with the Social Security Administration to ensure that you were reported as having a deferred vested benefit. Call the Social Security Administration toll-free at (800) 772-1213. Even if you don't request this information,

Social Security will automatically fill you in when you retire and apply for Social Security benefits. Still, I think it is a good idea to double-check after you leave your job. Stay in touch with the plan administrator, keeping him or her informed of any name or address changes to ensure that you will receive your full pension benefit.

I have read the literature about my pension and benefit accrual, but I don't really understand how it works. Can you explain it?

When you participate in a pension plan, you earn and accumulate—or accrue—pension benefits. Your accrued benefit is the amount that has been accumulated or allocated in your name under the plan as of a particular date. Plans can use any definition of service for the purpose of calculating your benefit accrual, as long as they use basically the same definition for all participants. Usually, a company calculates your years of service for purposes of benefit accrual from the date you became a plan participant, not necessarily from your date of hire.

If I work part-time, how are my years of service calculated?

Employees who work at least 1,000 hours per year but do not work full-time must be credited with a pro rata portion of the benefit that they would accrue if they were employed full-time. In other words, if your plan requires that employees work at least 2,000 hours of service per year for full benefit accrual but you work only 1,000 hours per year, you will be credited with 50 percent of the full benefit. Check your summary plan description to see exactly how your plan calculates service credit.

Can my plan reduce my future benefits?

Your employer may amend your plan to reduce the rate at which benefits accrue in the future. For example, a plan that pays $10 in monthly benefits at age 65 for each year of service up through 2005 can be amended to say that benefits for years of service beginning in 2007 will be credited at a rate of $8 each month. If you are participating in a defined-benefit plan, you must receive written notice of any significant reduction in the rate of future benefit accruals after the plan amendment is adopted and at least 15 days before the effective date of the plan amendment. That notice is supposed to describe the plan amendment and the date it becomes effective.

I was employed by one company for 15 years before leaving for a job that I thought would be terrific but which turned out to be a disaster. I'm pretty sure I'll be able to get my old job back, but what will happen to my service credit?

If a break in your employment lasts long enough, it can have serious consequences for your pension if you were not fully vested when you left. However, your accrued benefits are normally protected if you have a short break, usually less than five years. If you are actually planning a leave of absence, you need to examine the rules of your plan carefully so that you do not lose pension benefits unnecessarily.

When can I count on beginning to receive benefits from my qualified retirement plan?

According to the Employee Retirement Income Security Act, you must begin to receive plan payments from a qualified plan no later than the 60th day after the close of the plan year in which the last of the following events occurs:

1. you turn 65 (or the normal retirement age specified by your plan);
2. you have participated in your plan for at least 10 years; or
3. you terminate your service with the employer.

"Normal retirement age" is defined as the earlier of:

1. the age specified in the plan as normal retirement age; or
2. age 65 *or* the fifth anniversary of the employee's participation in the plan, whichever is later.

Normal retirement age is also the point at which a participant must become 100 percent vested in the plan. So, for most people, being 100 percent vested in a qualified retirement plan is the factor that determines normal retirement age. These rules apply for both defined-contribution plans and defined-benefit plans.

Does the type of plan I have affect when or how I can start receiving benefits if I want to access them before I reach normal retirement age?

Yes. Again, check your summary plan description for the specific details of your plan, but generally, there are several conditions under which your plan might allow you to begin receiving payments "early." A defined-benefit plan could permit earlier payments by, say, providing for early-retirement benefits, which might have additional eligibility requirements. A defined-benefit plan might also allow benefits to be paid out when you terminate your employment, suffer a disability, or die. Often, 401(k) plans allow you to withdraw some or all of your vested accrued benefit when you leave your job, reach age 59½, become disabled, retire, die, or suffer some other hardship that may be defined in the summary plan description. Profit-sharing or stock bonus plans may allow you to receive your vested accrued benefit after you leave your job, reach a specific age, become disabled, die, or after a specific number of years have elapsed.

Can my plan force me to start receiving benefits?

If the total value of your vested accrued benefit is greater than a specified minimum, the plan cannot force you to start receiving benefits before you reach the normal retirement age. If your vested accrued benefit is below that minimum, though, you might be required to take this money as soon as possible, often when you leave your job. If your plan is qualified, you must generally begin taking benefit payments by April 1 of the calendar year following the calendar year in which you reach age 70½, whether you want to or not.

Do I have any choice about how my benefits are paid out?

Your plan will establish the forms in which you can receive your benefits, but it usually offers a variety of options. If you have a defined-benefit plan and you are not married, by law your benefit must be made available at least in the form of a life annuity—equal monthly payments for the rest of your life. If you are married, your benefit choices must include monthly income to your spouse after your death. Some defined-benefit plans may also allow you to take all your benefits in a single payment. Most likely, you will have the right to choose any of these options.

I think I should have begun receiving my benefits already, but I'm not getting them. What can I do?

First of all, examine your summary plan description. All plans are required by law to provide participants with written instructions describing how to make benefit claims and how to appeal when claims are denied. If you don't understand the plan description or it doesn't include a procedure, write a letter making your claim directly to the plan administrator. If you make a claim for your benefit and it is rejected, your plan is required to notify you in writing of the rejection, along with specific reasons for the denial. In the denial letter, your plan is also required by law to explain how you can appeal the decision.

My plan administrator hasn't officially rejected my claim for benefits, but he keeps saying that my claim is still under review. How long can this go on?

Not for long—at least not legally. If your plan has a legitimate reason for needing additional time to examine your claim, they have to send you written notification within 90 days explaining why additional review time is necessary and giving you a date by which a decision is expected. If the plan is trying to deny or is delaying your claim because it needs information, they are required to inform you, in writing, of what information is needed. If you don't hear anything from the plan within 90 days of making your claim, legally you can appeal as though your claim had been officially denied.

Once my claim has been denied, how long do I have to appeal?

Again, check your summary plan description for details. Your plan is required to give you at least 60 days to appeal a denial, and the administrator is usually required to make a decision within 60 days of the appeal. If you find yourself in this situation, you should be communicating with the plan in writing and keeping copies of all correspondence. Just as in the initial review stage, the plan has to give you its decision, along with reasons for it, in writing.

What if the plan denies my claim again, but I know I'm entitled to my benefits?

At this point, you need to consult a lawyer; you may have to file a lawsuit. Now it is crucial that you complete all necessary stages of administrative appeal available before you turn to the courts. This is another reason for you to make sure you understand the rules in your specific plan and to keep careful records of all your communications regarding your benefits.

I worked for my company for many years without any problems. Then, out of the blue, I was fired. I suspect it was done so my employer could avoid paying my pension. Can they really do this?

No. It's illegal. Employers are absolutely not allowed to discharge, fine, suspend, expel, discipline, or discriminate against you or any of your beneficiaries for the purpose of interfering with any benefits that you are entitled to under their retirement plan, and they can be fined for doing so. If you think your employer is interfering with your benefits, consult a lawyer who has expertise in labor law and the Employee Retirement Income Security Act.

What will happen to my pension payments if I retire and then decide to go back to work?

What happens to your pension payments really depends on your particular plan. If you go back to work after you retire at a company other than the one from which you retired, in most cases, it will have no effect on the pension payments you have been receiving from the job you retired from.

What if I go back to work for the same employer?

It will depend on the arrangement you make at that time. If, for whatever reason, it has been agreed that your pension payments will stop when you go back to work for your original employer, the company must allow you to continue to accrue benefits until you meet the maximum total years of service that the plan will allow.

If you retired early and are receiving early-retirement benefits and then return to work for your original employer before you reach normal retirement age, some plans will suspend payment of your retirement benefits while you are reemployed. If your plan would *not* have suspended your benefits if you had returned to work after reaching normal retirement age, and the plan pays an actuarially reduced early-retirement benefit, then your plan has to recalculate your monthly payment when you retire again.

The bottom line is, if you are retired and are thinking about taking another job or returning to your old one, before you start working again, consult the rules of your plan to see if and how your pension benefits would be affected. Write to the plan administrator if you're not sure how your situation would be interpreted under the rules in your summary plan description.

EARLY RETIREMENT

In order to entice long-term, relatively well-paid employees to retire early, many companies offer them additional benefits such as an increased pension, the opportunity to receive the pension immediately, and health-care benefits. Another common inducement is to offer a lump-sum severance payment.

This section will help you decide whether to accept your company's early-retirement offer. Even if you do not have a choice, you should still read this section carefully—it contains vital information regarding what to do with the money in your retirement account as well as how to take your pension offer.

Once I decide to retire, how long do I have to decide what to do with the money in my retirement account?

Making a decision about retirement is stressful. Fortunately, you don't have to make all of your financial decisions at the same time. Most companies will allow you to leave your money in the company plan for at least a year after you retire, and many will allow you to leave your funds there until you turn 70½, at which time you must, by law, begin withdrawing the minimum required distribution. So don't feel pressured to make any decisions or move your money if you're not ready. Find out your company's deadlines. You probably have some time to think about what to do with your retirement account.

I've been told that when I retire I have to take all my money out of my 401(k) and roll it over into a single IRA account. Is that correct?

Absolutely not! Many people think that they have to roll over their entire retirement account into one place, but they are mistaken. Here are just a few options:

- If your company allows you to do so, you can leave your money in your 401(k).
- You can roll over all the money into one IRA.
- You can do an unlimited number of rollovers into as many IRAs as you want.
- You can leave some of your money in the company

plan (assuming that the company allows you to do this) and roll the rest of it over into one or more IRAs.

- If you are 55 or older in the year you retire, you can take distributions of all or part of your retirement account without penalty. You will still have to pay ordinary income tax on those distributions.
- If you were born before January 1, 1936, you may be able to take advantage of a favorable tax treatment known as ten-year averaging, which I explained earlier in this chapter.

Essentially, your options are leaving your money in the company plan, rolling it over into one or more IRAs, or doing a combination of both.

MONTHLY PENSION VS. LUMP-SUM PAYMENT

I'm about to leave the company that I've been working for, and I have been given two options. I can receive the money in my retirement plan in one lump sum, or the company will give me a monthly pension check for as long as I live. Which option should I take?

Whether you receive the money from your retirement plan in a lump-sum payment or as a monthly pension check depends on the following seven factors:

- How much you have in your retirement account.
- The amount of the monthly payment the company will give you.
- The amount of the monthly payment the company will pay to your spouse or life partner after you have died.

- Your age.
- Your life expectancy and the life expectancy of your spouse.
- Whether you need this income to live on.
- Whether this income needs to support another person after you have died.

To decide between taking your pension as a lump sum or as monthly payments, start by looking at the actual return you would get if you took the monthly pension payments and compare that to what you could reasonably expect to get on your own if you took a lump sum and invested it.

Let's say you are 60 years old and you are being offered a choice of $250,000 in one lump sum or $1,300 a month every month for the rest of your life. When you die, your life partner or spouse would receive half of the monthly pension ($650 a month).

To figure out the rate of return, we need to do some math. Take the monthly pension amount that your company is offering you and multiply it by 12. This is how much you will receive in pension payments annually ($1,300 × 12 = $15,600). Take that answer and divide it by the lump sum you are being offered ($15,600 ÷ $250,000 = .0624, or 6.24 percent). This answer is, in essence, the percentage return the company is giving you on your money.

Do these calculations again, this time using the amount that your surviving spouse or life partner will get ($650 × 12 = $7,800; $7,800 ÷ $250,000 = .0312, or 3.12 percent).

Now take your answers and fill them into the following paragraph:

Do you think that over your life expectancy you can earn _____ percent a year on your money without risk and that after you die your spouse or life partner could earn _____ percent?

Using the numbers in the example above, the paragraph would read like this:

Do you think that over your life expectancy you can earn 6.24 percent a year on your money without risk and that after you die your spouse or life partner could earn 3.12 percent?

If you can safely say that you could not, now or in the future, earn anywhere close to the interest rate the company is offering to pay you, you might be able to stop right here and take the monthly pension option. But if the numbers are close, and they probably will be, then it will pay for you to look at the other variables that go into this decision. Don't overlook the fact that with monthly pension payments, you no longer have the principal available for you or your beneficiaries.

What does age have to do with whether I take a pension or a lump-sum payment?

Age has a lot to do with your decision. If you choose a lump-sum payment, in order to delay having to pay income taxes on the money in your retirement account you will need to transfer this money into an IRA rollover, and IRA rollover accounts are governed by age restrictions. In most circumstances, you cannot easily touch these funds before age 59½. Also, by April 1 after the year you turn 70½, you have to start making mandatory withdrawals. Let's say you are only 56 years old, and you need the interest from this retirement money to live on. If you take the lump-sum payment and roll over the money, you will not be able to freely access these funds without penalty for another three and a half years, or until you reach age 59½. There are ways around this, such as SEPP (substantially equal periodic payments), but they are somewhat complicated. If this is the case, you may find that taking the monthly pension works better for you.

If you are older, your age still comes into play, because you have to start taking those mandatory distributions at age 70½. Let's say you are 65 years old and about to retire. You need all the income your retirement plan can generate. You opt for the lump-sum payment, put all the money into an IRA rollover, and buy a five-year Treasury note earning 6.5 percent. Your monthly income is $1,345, just about what they would give you as a monthly payment. You think you can't lose, since you will even have money left to leave your beneficiaries if you take the lump sum. But you must remember that when you hit age 70½, you have to start making mandatory withdrawals from that IRA account. This is because the government wants the tax money that you have deferred for so long on those funds. Over time, because of taxes, you may find that you do not have anywhere near that $250,000 you started with to generate interest for you. And if, when this happens, interest rates stagnate or decline, you may find yourself with significantly less income per month than if you had taken the monthly pension.

What if I choose to take a monthly pension, and then I go back to work and don't need the money? Do I still have to take the pension and pay taxes on it?

Yes. That is another reason you need to look at your situation very closely. If returning to work is at all a possibility for you, you are probably better off taking a lump-sum payment and rolling over the funds. If you end up not needing that money for income, you can invest it for growth. If you take the pension and then get another job, you are double-dipping—you are getting a salary and a pension at the same time. The problem is that you are getting money that you may not need, you must pay taxes on this money, and you are missing the opportunity to invest it for growth.

Will my pension increase over time?

Some monthly pensions are indexed for inflation, but many more are not. So please find out if your pension payment is indexed. This is yet another factor that you need to consider. If you invest a lump-sum payment wisely and interest rates go up, you could keep up with inflation—or maybe even outpace it. You will not be stuck with the frozen dollar amount of your monthly pension payment for the rest of your life. Keep in mind, however, that if interest rates go down and/or you have not invested your lump-sum payment wisely, you could see your income deteriorate.

Are there reasons other than how much I'm earning in interest on this money to take a lump-sum payment rather than the monthly pension?

Yes. Remember, when you take a monthly pension, depending on the payment option you choose, it may stop when you die. Even if it continues to be paid to your spouse or life partner after your death, upon his or her death it definitely stops. If you have children, this means they will get nothing. But if you took this money as a lump sum and invested it wisely, even with mandatory distributions starting at the age of 70½, you probably could still have money to pass on to your beneficiaries. If you are married or have a life partner and/or children, always look at all your options when it comes to joint and survivor benefits.

JOINT AND SURVIVOR BENEFITS

Can you explain joint and survivor benefits?

If you receive a basic pension when you retire, you usually

have the option of reducing your monthly pension in exchange for your spouse or life partner's continuing to receive some portion of your pension after you die. This is called a *joint and survivor option*, and you can often choose among several levels of joint and survivor benefits, usually 100 percent, 75 percent, 50 percent, and 25 percent. The larger the percentage of your monthly pension you want your spouse or life partner to get, the more money will be deducted from your basic pension each month. Federal law requires written permission from your spouse if you opt to take less than a 50 percent joint and survivor benefit on a tax-qualified plan, and some states require the same for noncompany plans, such as IRAs.

Are joint and survivor benefits only for married people?
Most people with access to joint and survivor benefits are married, but there are some companies that do allow joint and survivor benefits to unmarried and same-sex couples.

I plan to take the 50 percent option, since I don't think my wife will need as much money to live on after I am gone. Why not enjoy the money together while we can?
Most people do opt for the 50 percent joint and survivor benefit, thinking that their surviving spouse will need less to live on. I totally disagree with this logic. Most people are wrong about this, unfortunately, and their surviving spouses, in addition to being alone, are left struggling financially. Think about it. For married couples, when one spouse dies, the loss of one Social Security check can make a big financial difference. Also, if at the same time, the survivor's monthly pension check is cut by 50 percent, the financial results can be devastating. Remember, after your death, your spouse is all alone. Therefore, he or she may incur more expenses. If the deceased partner did a lot

of repair and maintenance work around the house or on the car, the surviving spouse may find himself or herself needing to hire—and pay—professionals to do that work. Also think about simple loneliness. You and your spouse may spend a lot of time at home together. But when one partner dies, the other partner is going to want and need to spend more time with friends and family members, and otherwise keep him- or herself occupied—which can cause his or her expenses to increase, not decrease.

All those possible increases are definitely scary. But we were careful to pay off the house before I retired, so I know my wife could always sell it if she had to. Isn't that a source of security?

It is. But although this is a common strategy, it has many potential problems. What if your partner doesn't want to sell the house? What if it takes longer to sell the house than you anticipated or if it doesn't sell for as much as you expect? Then where will your spouse be? Where will your spouse live after the house is sold? In all likelihood, the house you are living in now is the least expensive living situation available. And there are so many other factors aside from the financial value attached to your home. You don't want to put your spouse or partner in a situation where he or she is forced to sell the home just to pay bills.

What does the joint and survivor benefit cost if I choose to take it?

Each company has its own pricing system, and not all of them make a joint and survivor option affordable. You have to figure out if the options available from your company are cost-effective for you.

How do I decide whether the joint and survivor benefit my company is offering is cost-effective?

Use the following formula:

ITEM	J&S OPTIONS	EMPLOYEE	PARTNER BENEFIT	BENEFIT COST
1	Basic pension	A	B	C
2	50% option	D	E	F
3	100% option	G	H	I

BASIC PENSION

Under Item 1A, put the full monthly amount of your basic pension. This is how much you would receive each month if you took no joint and survivor option, and upon your death, your spouse will not receive anything. Under B put a zero, because your partner's benefit is nothing if you pass away first. Under C put a zero, because this option does not cost you a thing. The company owes you the basic pension, and you are not paying for any additional benefit.

50% OPTION

Under Item 2D, put the dollar amount that appears in the 50 percent joint and survivor section on your benefit statement. Take the figure you entered under D and divide it by two; put this figure under E. This is the benefit that your partner will receive each month after your death. Now subtract D from A. Put this figure under F. This is how much less you will receive from the 50 percent joint and survivor benefit while you're alive.

100% OPTION

Under Item 3G, put the dollar amount that appears in the 100 percent joint and survivor section of your benefit statement. Take whatever figure you have put under G under H as well. After your death, your spouse should receive the same monthly benefit that you were paid. Now subtract G from A and write that figure under I. This is how much the 100 percent joint and survivor option will cost you each month.

Once you have filled in the chart, the cost and benefit to you during your lifetime of each option should be clear (though if there is a significant age difference between you and your spouse, there are other options to consider; we'll discuss that in just a bit). It may make sense to multiply the numbers by 12 to get the yearly cost and benefit to you for each option. Then the question becomes: Is there any way to secure the same or better benefits for a surviving spouse or life partner for less money?

LIFE INSURANCE VS. JOINT AND SURVIVOR OPTION

Joint and survivor benefits seem kind of like a life insurance policy. Is that accurate?
In a way, yes. And it is a simple matter to compare the costs of various life insurance policies to what your company is charging for that 100 percent benefit. They may be significantly cheaper. If, for example, your basic pension amount would be decreased by at least half in order to have joint and survivor

benefits, that's expensive and you should be sure to compare the cost with other life insurance alternatives.

What happens if I receive these joint and survivor benefits and my spouse dies before I do?

In many cases, you will be stuck with those lower benefits for the rest of your life (in the sense that your pension remains reduced) even though no one is alive to use them after you die. This is a potential downside of the joint and survivor benefit option. Some companies offer something called a pop-up option (also known as a reinstatement of original benefits), which, for a small additional fee, allows you to have your basic pension amount reinstated if your spouse dies before you do. As a general rule, pop-up benefits are available only to married couples, even if the joint and survivor benefits are available to unmarried partners.

What should I look for in a life insurance policy as an alternative to joint and survivor benefits?

The most important thing to keep in mind about any insurance you buy as an alternative to joint and survivor benefits is to make sure that the policy will pay out a specific death benefit no matter how long the covered employee lives and regardless of any fluctuations in interest rates. Ask the insurance agent for an example of the guaranteed values of the policy. These should show you what the minimum death benefit would be no matter what happens with interest rates. That way you can see what could happen in the worst-case situation.

What are the advantages of purchasing a life insurance policy vs. the joint and survivor benefit option?

A life insurance policy offers you a tax advantage, because after the insured partner dies, the death benefit passes as a lump sum to the beneficiary, income tax–free. With the joint and survivor option, the surviving spouse receives the income in smaller, taxable monthly payments, and may see more and more of that monthly benefit go to taxes if his or her tax bracket becomes higher. The lump-sum life insurance proceeds also could be invested in tax-free bonds, which would make any income generated by them tax-free, too. Another advantage of life insurance is that you can invest the proceeds to take advantage of changes in interest rates, a hedge against inflation that a pension won't provide (unless your pension has a cost-of-living increase). If your spouse dies first, the life insurance policy can be discontinued and you can withdraw the cash value. Finally, if you, the policyholder, die first, and your surviving spouse inherits the life insurance proceeds and invests wisely, when he or she dies those proceeds, or what remains of them, can be passed on to other beneficiaries, whereas the joint and survivor benefit would simply stop being paid.

Which joint and survivor option do you like best?

The 100 percent joint and survivor benefit is probably the most cost-effective and beneficial option, even if initially it seems expensive. But explore the alternatives with a professional adviser, because, depending on the particular details of your company's options and your individual financial situation, health, and age, there could be a better choice for you.

If I have decided to take the joint and survivor benefit, is there any time that it is OK to take less than the 100 percent option?

Yes, and here are the exceptions:

- You are absolutely guaranteed to receive a significant inheritance or windfall in the immediate future that will take care of your spouse or life partner's needs no matter what.

- Your nonworking partner is significantly older than you are, or has a serious or terminal illness. In either of these situations, it may seem to make sense to take the basic pension, in which case your spouse will not receive anything, because you assume that your spouse will die first. I think this strategy can be risky, though. What if you were the victim of a freak car accident, and your much older or ill spouse survived you, only to live—maybe for years—with no income?

What is the best way for a married person to deal with this kind of situation, if taking the basic pension without the survivor benefit is never a safe option?

Remember the pop-up option that we discussed earlier? Well, if your company offers such an option, these are excellent circumstances in which to use it. You can take the 100 percent joint and survivor option, and if your partner or spouse dies first, as seems likely, you can return to the basic pension amount and not have to continue paying for a benefit that your partner will never use. This is optimal protection for both of you.

What if my company does not offer a pop-up option?

Depending on your age and your health, term life insurance (only in this particular scenario) may be a relatively inexpensive alternative. If you know that, without a shadow of a doubt, your partner has no chance of living beyond the term of the life insurance policy, you can consider this option seriously. This strategy has the added benefit of possibly resulting in some additional money to leave your children, for example, if you died unexpectedly and your partner died shortly thereafter. The main benefit, of course, is that your partner would be protected in the event of your death.

Why can't I just take my basic pension and invest part of it on my own to accumulate the money my spouse will need in 20 or 30 years? Isn't that really what the company is doing with my money anyway?

I understand how you feel, but let me tell you why I don't recommend this strategy. Investing responsibly on your own for 20 years or more might be an alternative if you could forecast the day you're going to die. But, of course, you don't know when that is going to happen, and it is very possible that you won't have enough time to accumulate the money that your partner will need. For your partner's sake, do not tempt fate.

CIVIL SERVICE RETIREMENT BENEFITS

What are civil service retirement benefits?

A large number of Americans have been or are currently employed by agencies and departments of the federal government. Jobs in the civil service often pay less than comparable jobs in the private sector, but they do have one great advantage, and that is a very comprehensive retirement system. In fact, there are two federal retirement systems, the Civil Service Retirement System (CSRS) and the Federal Employees Retirement System (FERS).

What is the difference between the Civil Service Retirement System and the Federal Employees Retirement System?

Until 1984, every federal government worker in this country was part of the Civil Service Retirement System. Unless they had also worked in the private sector, these workers were not covered by the U.S. Social Security system. Starting January 1, 1984, any worker hired by the federal government has been made a part of a different plan, the Federal Employees Retirement System. These workers are insured by Social Security.

What kinds of benefits are government employees hired before 1984 eligible for?

In 1984, federal employees were given the option of remaining in the old system, the Civil Service Retirement System, or changing over to the Federal Employees Retirement System. Both programs are administered by the U.S. government's Office of Personnel Management, known as the OPM, and both are funded by employees' payroll deductions, as well as by contributions from federal agencies. Both systems offer disability, retirement, and survivors benefits. But neither the CSRS nor the FERS offers dependents benefits. The benefits are based on the worker's highest average salary for any three consecutive years of employment.

How do I know if I am eligible for either the CSRS or the FERS?

You are considered eligible if you have worked for at least five years for the U.S. government as a civilian employee. This means that you can qualify for a government pension, also known as a retirement annuity. Also, if you have worked for at least five years as a federal civilian employee, you are eligible to get retirement credit for any years after 1956 that you served in the military, provided you pay a premium based on the amount of your military pay.

What kind of retirement benefits are offered by the CSRS and the FERS?

There are two kinds of retirement annuities offered under the CSRS and the FERS. One is an immediate annuity, and the other is a deferred annuity. An annuity is a type of investment that an insurance company invests on your behalf (see *Ask Suze . . . About Mutual Funds and Annuities*).

What are my choices for taking my retirement benefits?

If you have worked for the federal government for at least five years, you are eligible to retire at age 62. At this point, you have a choice: You can immediately begin to receive an annuity paid out of your retirement account, to which you have contributed through payroll deductions. (Again, the five years that you worked for the federal government do not necessarily have to be consecutive, nor do you have to have served five years in the same department.) Alternatively, you may take all of the money from your retirement account at once.

If you stop working for the federal government before you have reached the age of retirement, you cannot begin to withdraw your annuity immediately. You can leave the money that has accumulated in your CSRS or FERS account, or you can withdraw it in a lump sum. If you leave it in the account, you are deferring your annuity payments until age 62—that's why it's called a deferred annuity. If you change your mind and decide to withdraw your money before retirement, you can receive all of it in a lump sum anytime before you reach the age of 62.

Which option is preferable?

It will depend on how much monthly annuity income you are eligible for, compared with the income that your lump-sum withdrawal could generate if invested. If the monthly annuity sum is 2 or 3 percent above what the lump sum would generate, take the monthly annuity income. Otherwise, roll over the lump sum, invest the money on your own, and withdraw the income as needed.

My husband has worked for the federal government for 23 years. Is he entitled to any special benefits?

Because your spouse has worked at least 20 years in a federal job, he is eligible to claim his immediate annuity at the slightly younger age of 60. This is just the tip of the iceberg as far as duration of service in federal employment is concerned. A worker who has served in a federal government job for 30 years or more, and who is covered by the CSRS or the FERS, is eligible to retire with a pension at age 55. (As of 2002, however, this minimum retirement age began rising at the rate of two months per year for both CSRS and FERS.)

What happens if I am laid off from my federal government job before I become eligible for my pension?

The CSRS and the FERS both have rules in place that will permit some, though not all, long-term workers to take an immediate annuity even if they are laid off before retirement age. If an employee is covered under the CSRS and has been working for at least one year in the two years immediately preceding the date on which he or she was laid off, and is age 50 with 20 years of service (or any age with at least 25 years of service), that worker may be eligible to collect an immediate annuity.

One difference in eligibility requirements for a comparable worker covered by FERS is that he or she does not need to have been employed for one year before he or she was laid off. Another difference is that if the FERS employee claims his immediate annuity before he or she reaches age 55, the amount of annuity is not reduced for age. Under the CSRS, the annuity is reduced by ⅙ of 1 percent for each full month under the age of 55 at retirement.

My husband is an air traffic controller. Are the rules for his job different from those for other government workers?

Yes. The federal government, noting the high-stress nature of such jobs as air traffic controller and firefighter, as well as most law enforcement jobs, makes it easier for workers in these jobs to claim early retirement. The government also has lowered the minimum number of years that a worker in one of these fields has to serve in his or her job to receive a pension. If you are a police officer or a firefighter who is covered under CSRS, for example, you are permitted to claim your retirement benefits at age 50. If your husband, the air traffic controller, is covered by the CSRS and he has been at his job for 20 years or longer, he can retire at age 50. If he has been working 25 years at his job, then he is eligible for his retirement benefits at any time.

How do the CSRS and the FERS calculate my benefits?

Both systems use a variety of factors. The first is how long you have worked and how long you have been making contributions to the retirement fund. A second and equally important factor that both the CSRS and the FERS use to calculate the amount of your retirement annuity is what is known as a worker's *high-three average salary*.

What is a high-three average salary?

This represents an employee's average salary over the three consecutive years in which the worker received the highest amount of compensation. Both the CSRS and the FERS base the retirement annuity that they will pay a worker on this high-three average salary, but the way each calculates the benefit is different.

How does the CSRS perform its calculations?

The CSRS starts with your high-three average salary. To that number, say $40,666, it adds 1.5 percent of your high-three average pay and multiplies it by 5 (for your first five years of service). Then it adds 1.75 percent of your high-three average pay, times the number of years between five and nine that you have been employed as well as the number of years of total service. Finally, it adds 2 percent of your high-three average pay, multiplied by the number of years more than ten that you have been employed. The grand total is your retirement annuity.

How does the FERS calculate benefits?

The FERS calculates your retirement annuity by taking 1 percent of your high-three average and multiplying this number by the number of years you have spent in your job. You are also eligible to take early retirement under the FERS system (for a reduced benefit) if you have worked for ten or more years at your federal government job.

KEY RETIREMENT AND ESTATE PLANNING RULES

IRA/ROTH

MAXIMUM ANNUAL CONTRIBUTIONS

YEAR	UNDER 50 YEARS OF AGE	YEAR	50 AND OVER
2006–2007	$4,000		
2008	$5,000*	2006–2007	$5,000
		2008	$6,000*

*All amounts thereafter indexed for inflation in increments of $500.

401(K)/403(B)/457**

MAXIMUM ANNUAL CONTRIBUTIONS

YEAR	UNDER 50 YEARS OF AGE	50 AND OVER
2006	$15,000	$20,000
2007	$15,500	$20,500

**For government 457 plans, a special catch-up rule applies if you are three or fewer years away from retirement, letting you contribute up to twice the annual maximum amount in any given year.

SIMPLE

MAXIMUM ANNUAL CONTRIBUTIONS

YEAR	UNDER 50 YEARS OF AGE	50 AND OVER
2006	$10,000	$12,500
2007	$10,500	$13,000

REDUCTION IN INDIVIDUAL INCOME-TAX RATE***

YEAR	10% RATE	15% RATE	28% RATE REDUCED TO	31% RATE REDUCED: TO	36% RATE REDUCED TO	39.6% RATE REDUCED TO
May 6, 2003–2010	10%	15%	25%	28%	33%	35%

***Due to a "sunset" provision in the law, in 2011 income tax rates are due to revert to their year 2001 levels: 10%, 15%, 28%, 31%, 36%, and 39.6%.

MAXIMUM ESTATE AND GIFT-TAX RATES****

YEAR	ESTATE-TAX EXEMPTION	GIFT-TAX EXEMPTION	HIGHEST ESTATE- AND GIFT-TAX RATE
2006	$2 million	$1 million	46%
2007	$2 million	$1 million	45%
2008	$2 million	$1 million	45%
2009	$3.5 million	$1 million	45%
2010	Estate Tax Repealed		Top individual income-tax rate (gift tax only)

****Due to a "sunset" provision, in 2011 the maximum estate-tax rate is due to revert to 55%.

FINANCING COLLEGE EDUCATION

In recent years a few welcome developments have made it easier to pay for college. One is a federal push to make college more affordable, which includes new educational tax credits, federally sponsored IRAs that promote saving for college, and new deductions for interest paid on student loans (For more about student loan interest deductions, please see Ask *Suze . . . About Debt.*) Second, new state-sponsored college savings plans have proliferated, and many of these now work in your favor, from both an investment and a tax-savings standpoint. Third, college officials are acknowledging that higher education has become wildly expensive and, without help, increasingly unaffordable to all but a few. According to the College Board, in the 2006–2007 school year the average cost of tuition, room and board, books and supplies, transportation, and other expenses at a public four-year college was $15,600, while the average cost at a private four-year college was $32,000. Colleges and universities are beginning to offer more aid to help defray these costs. The latest figures show 63 percent of undergraduate students were awarded some form of financial aid, including 52 percent of students who came from households with annual incomes of $92,000 or more.

Still, parents have to be careful when choosing from the menu of available options, since how you put together your college savings package can affect your eligibility for financial aid. The details—whether you're married or divorced, live in Montana or New York, have a child who's gifted, or invest in an UGMA account—matter in determining how much you will have to spend, and how much you can save, when you want to provide for your child's higher education.

Even if you're starting late, don't worry. The important point is to start. Read the following questions and answers, and begin with a few simple actions. Open a Roth or an Education IRA. Sign up for a 529 plan. Check out websites devoted to financial aid, and gather further information about everything on the website *www.savingforcollege.com*. There is more support and there are more options out there than you may be aware of.

INVESTING FOR EDUCATION

What do you think is the best way to invest money to finance a child's education?

Your investment strategy will depend on how many years you have ahead of you before your child or children enter college. Whenever you're considering how to invest, the period of time in which you can allow your money to remain invested for growth is a critical factor. If you have a minimum of ten years before your first child enters college, I suggest investing in growth stocks, growth mutual funds, or exchange-traded funds (ETFs). In the shorter term, however, the ups and downs of stocks can be a problem. During a sudden downturn in the market, if you had to cash in your stocks for a tuition payment you could lose not only your gains but also some of your principal. If you know you'll need to begin spending your savings within four or five years, be conservative. Keep your money in high-yield money-market funds, Treasury notes, certificates of deposit, and series EE bonds. If you have a little more time than this—say, six to seven years—and feel you can tolerate a moderate amount of risk, consider using not all but a portion of your money to invest for growth.

In what kind of plan or account should I be keeping my investments for a child's education?

Where you hold your investments is just as important as the kind of investments you decide to make. Should you keep them in your name or in your child's name? Should they be held in a UGMA account, an Education IRA, a prepaid tuition plan, a 529 savings plan, or a Roth IRA? Since there are many choices, let's go through them one at a time.

UNIFORM GIFTS TO MINORS ACT/UNIFORM TRANSFERS TO MINORS ACT (UGMA/UTMA)

UGMA, or the Uniform Gifts to Minors Act, and UTMA, or the Uniform Transfers to Minors Act, were created to make tax-free gifting of money or assets to children easier and more efficient. As a parent, you can open either an UGMA or an UTMA account in your child's name. (Grandparents and friends of the family can open accounts as well.) You fund it with gifts of money, and then, if you wish, you can purchase stocks, bonds, annuities, or other investment vehicles with the balance. UGMA and UTMA accounts are governed under the laws of the state where the account is set up, but generally, you or an adult delegate serves as the account custodian until your child reaches the age of majority (18 or 21, depending on the state), at which point he or she controls the money.

With either account, annual taxes on the gains, or unearned income (such as dividends, interest, and capital gains), are negligible until total gains in the account reach $1,700. After that, the gains are taxed at the parents' highest marginal income-tax rate—that is, until the child reaches age 18, when gains begin to be taxed at the child's lower rate.

Given the greater tax advantages of the new federal Coverdell Education Savings Accounts (see page 120) and of Section 529 college-savings plans (see page 135), both of which let parents or guardians hold the money saved for college in the parents' or guardians' name, UGMA and UTMA accounts are much less attractive than they used to be as a method of saving for children's college education. That said, virtually every bank and stock brokerage firm (full-service, discount, and online) manages these accounts on a daily basis. You should be able to set up an account with any major institution.

Are there any differences between UGMA and UTMA?

Yes, one significant difference. Though in most ways UTMA and UGMA accounts are alike, UTMA has this benefit: It may allow you, the parent, to maintain control over the account for a slightly longer period of time—until, for example, your child finishes college. Unlike the regulations governing UGMA, those governing UTMA permit the custodian to postpone final distribution of the account funds until the child reaches age 25, depending on the state in which the account is set up. This is important, especially if you think your child may put off attending college, may wish to attend graduate school after college, or may not wish to attend college or graduate school at all. In some states, the child can do whatever he or she wishes with the money in an UGMA account once he or she reaches age 18—go skiing, form a rap group, or support an unappealing significant other. In all states, the money is irrevocably the child's once he or she reaches 21. Over the years, I have seen many UGMA accounts that were supposed to fund a college education go instead to buying a new car or supporting a drug or alcohol habit, while the parents had to watch, brokenhearted and powerless to intervene. This is one major potential drawback of saving in either an UGMA or an UTMA account, but at least an UTMA delays the risk.

Can you elaborate on the tax benefits of saving in an UGMA/UTMA account rather than in an account held in my own name?

Yes. The potential tax savings can be significant, thanks to the difference between income-tax brackets for adults and those for children.

Here are some examples, based on tax laws as of the year 2006:

- The first $850 of unearned income in a minor's UGMA/UTMA account is exempt from tax—regardless of the child's age.
- The second $850 of unearned income from securities given to a child is taxed according to the minor's tax bracket—again, regardless of the minor's age.
- The child's age becomes a factor only when unearned income exceeds $1,700. If the child is younger than age 18 at the close of the tax year in which gains have exceeded that limit, investment income over $1,700 is taxed at the parents' highest marginal rate. Such income must be included on either the parents' tax return or a separate return. Since certain deductions may be available only to the child, filing a separate return for this income may result in lower taxes. If the minor reaches the age of 18 at any time during the year when gains on the account exceed $1,700, all income in excess of $850 is taxed at the child's rate.

Will an UGMA account make it harder for my child to qualify for financial aid?

Yes, and this is the second potential drawback of using UGMA/UTMA to save for college. Because an UGMA/

UTMA account is held in your child's name, funding it can seriously reduce your child's chances of qualifying for aid. Let's say, for example, that the annual tuition of the school that your dependent daughter wants to attend is $8,000, and that apart from your home and retirement savings, you and your spouse have assets of $30,000 in your name. Under these circumstances, the college would expect you to contribute 6 percent of that $30,000, or $1,800, per year for your daughter's college expenses. The remainder might possibly be paid with the help of some form of financial aid. If the same $30,000 were held in an UGMA account in your daughter's name, however, the college would expect you to use these funds at the rate of 35 percent, or $10,500, per year for college expenses. That's a big difference! When you consider paying $10,500 from an UGMA rather than $1,800 from your own account, it's easy to grasp one of the fundamental weaknesses of a savings strategy based on UGMA/UTMA.

Are there other ways to put money aside for college and also get the child's-rate tax advantage of an UGMA/UTMA?

Yes, so read on. However, if you plan to put money aside for your children's education, please consider keeping it in a separate account in your own name. The advantages of doing so include ongoing control of the money and a better chance of qualifying for financial aid.

EDUCATION TAX BENEFITS/CREDITS

EDUCATION TAX BENEFITS/CREDITS

The government provides one new tax deduction and two federal tax credits to help you finance your children's educations. The tax credits are called the Hope Scholarship and the Lifetime Learning Credit.

Who qualifies for the new tax deduction?

Many people can deduct up to $4,000 of higher-education expenses from their income each year for tax purposes. To be eligible, adjusted gross income for a single filer must be $80,000 or less, and for joint filers must be $160,000 or less.

What is the Hope Scholarship?

The Hope Scholarship is a relatively new, generous tax credit that allows you to deduct as much as $1,650 a year directly from your income-tax bill for every college freshman and sophomore in the family. Remember, a credit is not deducted from your income for tax purposes; it is deducted directly from the amount of the tax you pay, and therefore is far more valuable. The Hope Scholarship credit is divided into two parts: You can deduct 100 percent of the first $1,100 of a child's tuition (but not the cost of room and board or books, and not for courses involving sports, games, or hobbies, unless the courses are part of the student's degree requirements), and 50 percent of the next $1,100 in tuition. The Hope Scholarship is claimed on a per-student basis, so if you are the parents of two sets of twins, all college freshmen and sophomores, you can claim up to $1,650 a year for each of them.

What is the Lifetime Learning Credit?

The Lifetime Learning Credit is a smaller credit for parents of students in their junior year of college and beyond, for which you can reap tax savings of up to $2,000 a year. You can deduct 20 percent of the first $10,000 of out-of-pocket costs for qualified tuition and related expenses for all the students in the family, up to a maximum of $2,000 per family per year.

Just as the Hope Scholarship runs out, students become eligible for the Lifetime Learning Credit. But the Lifetime Learning Credit is a per-family, not a per-student, credit. It applies to all the children for whom you're paying educational expenses out of your pocket.

You should be aware that both the Hope Scholarship and the Lifetime Learning Credit are phased out for taxpayers with modified adjusted gross income above specified levels, based on filing status. In 2007, the income ranges for the phase-out are $97,000 to $114,000 for married couples filing jointly, and $47,000 to $57,000 for single parents. Married taxpayers filing separately are not eligible for the credits.

EDUCATION SAVINGS ACCOUNTS

What is a Coverdell Education Savings Account?

Before the Economic Growth and Tax Relief Reconciliation Act of 2001, this tax-advantaged college-savings program was widely known as the Education IRA. It was specifically created to help parents and others fund a child's education. The act changed this program's name to the Coverdell Education Savings Account, and it improved it in a variety of ways. In the past, the largest contribution that could be made to an Education IRA was $500 per child (or beneficiary) per year. The maximum contribution to the Education Savings Account is now $2,000 per child. The act also raised the maximum adjusted gross income (AGI) level of married couples who wish to contribute to an Education Savings Account, and extended it so that it can now also be used to fund elementary- and secondary-school expenses, such as private-school tuition. The child must be under the age of 18 when contributions are made. The contribution is not tax-deductible and does not have any effect on the amount you can contribute to traditional IRAs, Roth IRAs, or combinations of the two.

Who can set up an Education Savings Account?

Anyone who meets the AGI requirements can set up and fund an Education Savings Account for a specific child. The contributor does not have to be a parent or relative, only someone who wants to provide for a child's education. To contribute the maximum each year, the contributor's AGI cannot be more than $95,000 a year if he or she files taxes singly, or $190,000 if he or she is married and files jointly. The maximum amount of the contribution is reduced as income rises above those levels and is phased out completely once an AGI reaches $110,000 for single filers and $220,000 for couples.

I am a grandparent who wants to set up an Education Savings Account for my grandchild, but my income comes from my pension and interest on investments. Even though I am not employed and do not draw a salary, can I still set up an account?

Yes, you can. Unlike a Roth IRA or a traditional IRA, the Education Savings Account doesn't place restrictions on the source of money used to fund it. In this way, the law makes it possible for grandparents—and possibly even the children themselves—to make contributions.

How are distributions from an Education Savings Account taxed?

Distributions from an Education Savings Account are not subject to tax if used for "qualified higher-education expenses," and as long as the Hope Scholarship and the Lifetime Learning Credit are not used in the same year for the same educational expenses for which the distributions are used. This means that the earnings, or gains, on your contributions will never be taxed if the funds are properly used. However, ordinary income taxes and a 10 percent penalty can be slapped on earnings if distributions are used for anything other than qualified education expenses.

When must all the money in an Education Savings Account be distributed?

All funds in an Education Savings Account must be distributed before the beneficiary reaches age 30. However, if the primary beneficiary reaches that age and hasn't used the funds in the account to pay for college or advanced education, the account can be transferred to another beneficiary without tax or penalty if that person and the first beneficiary are members of the same family.

If I am already making a contribution to a state tuition program, can I also set up an Education Savings Account?

Yes. You can fund both a qualified state tuition program, such as a Section 529 plan, and an Education Savings Account in the same year for the same child. When it comes to taking *distributions,* however, be aware that combined distributions from an Education Savings Account and a qualified state tuition program cannot exceed a child's qualified educational expenses for any one year.

Should the Education Savings Account be my first choice to fund my child's education?

Probably. Since you can contribute up to $2,000 a year to the Education Savings Account, you'll be able to amass about $91,000 over an 18-year period, assuming an average annual 10 percent return on your money. This amounts to 60 percent of projected four-year private-college tuition costs in the year 2010.

Second, earnings in an Education Savings Account are currently tax-free when used for elementary- and secondary-school and college expenses, so the tax savings can be significant. Also, you can now take advantage of the Education Savings Account without forfeiting use of the Hope Scholarship or the Lifetime Learning Credit, as you would have had to do before 2002, if your income permits you to use these credits. You should be aware that both these advantages— along with the higher annual contribution of $2,000, raised from $500 in 2001—are set to expire in 2011, unless Congress acts to extend them.

Another concern is that money in an Education Savings Account may make it harder for your child to qualify for financial aid.

Note: There are other ways to save for a child's education, and one of them is a Roth IRA. (See page 39 for a full definition.)

Using a Roth IRA to Fund
a College Education

You say you like the Roth IRA as a saving vehicle for college. Why is that?

The Roth IRA, normally used as a vehicle for retirement saving, also can be a terrific way to save for college, although, like the Education Savings Account, your contributions are made with money on which you've already paid taxes. The Roth lets you save more money than an Education Savings Account does, and this yearly amount increases through the year 2008. (Please see page 111.) Second, you can withdraw your original contributions (though not your earnings) at any time for any purpose, without owing taxes or penalties. Finally, not only can you qualify for a Hope Scholarship or Lifetime Learning Credit while your child is receiving Roth IRA distributions, your child may have a better chance of qualifying for financial aid than with an Education Savings Account.

Can you give me an example of how a Roth IRA would work to help fund a child's education?

Yes. Say you are 30 years old and have a child. As part of a plan to save for the education of this child, you put the maximum amount allowed each year into a Roth IRA in your name. For the next 18 years, you continue to add the yearly maximum allowed to the Roth IRA, and you get an average annual return of 10 percent on your contributions. When your child is 18, you will have approximately $190,000 in your Roth IRA. You will be 48 years old—not so far from your own retirement. You will be able to take out your original contributions of $81,000 to help pay for your child's education (or, for that matter, for any other purpose) without penalties or taxes. That's only $10,000 less than you would have amassed in an Education IRA at $2,000 a year for 18 years at 10 percent. And remember, the laws governing a Roth IRA allow you to withdraw your original contributions at any time, for any reason, whether or not your child ever goes to college. Finally, after you take out your original $81,000, you will still have almost $109,000 in earnings remaining in the account, and that money will continue to grow income tax–free. It will never be taxed at all if you leave it in the Roth IRA until you turn age 59½ and have waited at least five years from the time you first began funding the account.

Who is eligible to fund a Roth?

As with the Education Savings Account, eligibility for a Roth has an income cap. To contribute the maximum allowed per year, the contributor's AGI cannot be more than $95,000 for those filing singly and $150,000 for those filing jointly. The contribution is phased out for those earning more than these amounts and is eliminated altogether when AGI reaches $110,000 for single filers and $160,000 for joint filers.

I want to use additional savings vehicles while my child is young. If I open a Roth IRA, will I be able to fund a 529 plan in that same year?

Yes. You can fund both a Roth IRA in your name and a Section 529 plan for your child in the same year.

Will a Roth reduce my child's chances of qualifying for financial aid, as an UGMA account can?

No. Because a Roth is primarily a retirement-savings vehicle, the money in your Roth will not make it harder for your child to qualify for financial aid.

PREPAID TUITION PLANS

What is a prepaid tuition plan?

Prepaid tuition plans are just what they sound like. You invest in the plan, and your investment buys a certain number of tuition credits at your state's college or university system at today's prices. Thus, no matter what increases take place in state tuition rates in future years, the number of semesters or years you have purchased for your child today is guaranteed. You select the number of years of college you want to purchase, the type of college (two- or four-year college), and a payment plan to fit your family's budget. The size of your payments will be determined by your child's age or grade—in other words, by how many years there are left before he or she is ready for college. When your child goes to college in the future, the plan will pay the full in-state tuition and mandatory fees at any public college in your state.

Who is eligible to invest in a prepaid plan?

The rules vary from state to state, but typically anyone with an interest in the educational future of a child—including a parent, grandparent, aunt, uncle, friend, or employer—can enroll and invest. An adult enrolls by buying a contract. To be eligible to buy a contract, you *or* the child on whose behalf you're investing must be a resident of the state at the time of enrollment. A parent or grandparent can purchase a contract in the state of Maryland for a child who lives in Maryland, for example, even if the parent or grandparent is a resident of Florida.

Is there an age limit for the beneficiary?

Again, this depends on the state. Many states, in an effort to make sure that the child in question is not too close to college age when the plan is purchased, impose an age limit.

I live in Maryland. Can you give me an example of how my state plan might work?

Yes. If you had enrolled in the Maryland Prepaid College Trust in the year 2006, you would have signed a contract stating that your payments would be based on the cost of tuition and mandatory fees for the 2005–2006 academic year. Later, when your child goes off to college, the plan would pay benefits based on the cost of the selected college at the time you signed your contract. Each year, the cost of college continues to rise. For example, in 1996 the tuition and mandatory fees at the University of Maryland's College Park campus were $4,169 for an in-state, full-time student. By 2001, these costs had increased to $5,341, and for the 2006–2007 academic year, tuition and mandatory fees increased to $7,906—a 90 percent increase in just 10 years. The plan invests your payments based on its projections that tuition will increase by an average of 7 percent each year, and that mandatory fees will increase at a rate of 10 percent a year.

In general, when you apply for a prepaid plan you are told how much your total payments will be to purchase one semester to five years of college, based on the age or grade of the child now. For example, if your child was in the fourth grade and you paid for four years of university tuition in Maryland using the five-year monthly payment option, your total payments to the plan would be $44,520. This is more than half of the projected tuition cost beginning in 2014, your fourth-grader's freshman year in college, which is $63,850.

Can my payments qualify as a gift under federal law?

Yes. The Internal Revenue Code provides that payments to a prepaid tuition plan are a "completed gift" for federal gift-tax purposes. The code also provides for a five-year averaging provision for individuals who contribute amounts greater than $12,000 ($24,000 for married couples) in a given taxable year. So total gifts of $60,000 per individual ($120,000 for married couples) are allowed in one tax year without federal gift-tax consequences.

When I use the money in my prepaid tuition plan for my child to go to college, can I also use the Hope Scholarship and/or Lifetime Learning Credit that same year?

Yes. The Hope Scholarship and the Lifetime Learning Credit can be used at the time that the tuition benefit is being paid to a college or university. However, other federally mandated guidelines, including the parents' income and the student's year in college, govern who may take advantage of these credits.

Are there tax incentives to invest in a prepaid tuition plan?

Yes. The earnings portion of these plans are entirely exempt from federal taxes, as they are in 529 plans (please see page 135). Earnings here are defined as the difference between the benefit paid to the college and your original contributions. Typically, you owe no state tax on the earnings when benefits are paid to a college. In most cases, all state taxes on the earnings in the plan are deferred while the money remains in the plan. Also, depending on your state, you may be able to deduct payments from your annual income for each contract you have purchased up to that state's limit. Payments in excess of the state limits per contract can be deducted from your income in future years, until the full amount of your payments has been deducted. Changes in your state or federal tax laws could alter the tax treatment of state prepaid tuition programs, so stay tuned.

What happens if I put money into a prepaid tuition plan and my child does not go to college, or she receives a scholarship? Can I get my money back? Will I owe taxes on the money I get back?

In general, you can get your money back if your child receives a grant or scholarship for benefits that would otherwise have been paid to a college by your plan. If your child were to suffer a death or disability prior to enrollment in college, you would receive your payments plus the investment return for the period of time the money was in the plan.

If your child does not attend college for reasons other than death or disability, you will receive a reduced refund plus half of the investment return for the period the money was in the plan. (If there's a loss, it would be minus that amount.) If your child has enrolled in college but does not finish all the years you paid for, you will receive a refund equal to the benefits that would have been paid to the college.

If the contract is less than three years old and you cancel, you will receive the payments you have made up until that point.

If the contract has been in existence for three years or more, you will receive your payments plus (or minus) half of the investment return for the time the money was in the fund.

All refunds are subject to taxes. Any portion of a refund in excess of contract payments (in other words, the earnings on the investment) is subject to state and federal taxation at your tax rate.

Any state deduction previously taken on your contributions would have to be added back into your income.

What are the limitations of prepaid plans?

In my estimation, there are three important limitations:

- The first is that you are paying for your child to go to a state school. What if he or she doesn't want to attend a state school? This is a possibility you have to consider. Some plans allow you to transfer your funds to an out-of-state college or university, but at a much reduced benefit.
- Second, these are prepaid *tuition* plans, which means that you prepay only tuition—not room and board or the cost of books and computers, which can make up a significant part of an education bill.
- Finally, your investment grows merely at the rate at which your school's tuition costs increase. If you invest in a prepaid plan, you win only when the tuition costs of the college you choose rise more quickly than the annual rate of return you might be earning in other investment vehicles.

PREPAID TUITION PLANS FOR PRIVATE COLLEGES

I've heard about a new prepaid 529 plan for private colleges and universities. What can you tell me about it?

The 529 plan you are referring to is called the Independent 529 plan. The Independent 529 plan is sponsored by a group of currently about 250-plus private colleges and universities across the country known as the consortium. The program manager is TIAA-CREF Tuition Financing Inc. (TFI). The way it works is very simple: You deposit a sum of money, which buys you what is known as a tuition certificate. This certificate is redeemable toward tuition at the colleges that are members of the consortium. So in essence you are purchasing a percentage of future tuition for each program year. For instance, let's say you make a $5,000 up-front contribution. This $5,000 may buy 30 percent of future tuition and mandatory fees at College A and 50 percent of future tuition and mandatory fees at College B. Certificates may be redeemed for college anytime between 36 months and 30 years after purchase. The percentages are set by the participating colleges at the time the tuition certificates are issued, and may not be adjusted later on. Each college is required to "discount" its tuition by at least one-half percent in setting its percentages. This contrasts with many state prepaid programs that are now charging premiums over current tuition levels.

How would I know what school my child is going to attend when my child is just a few years old?

When you first purchase a certificate of deposit, you will be asked to identify five "favorite" colleges to use as a gauge to illustrate how your account is performing. You can alter your selection of the five "favorite" colleges at any time. Quarterly you will receive statements that will show how much tuition you have purchased for each favorite, based on the college's tuition and certificate discount rate.

Will more private college or private university options be available by the time my child goes to college?

The Independent 529 plan expects more private colleges and

private universities will join in the future. When your beneficiary redeems their certificates, they can use them at any participating college, including colleges that join after the certificate of deposit has been purchased.

Is there a minimum contribution requirement or maximum contribution limit for the Independent 529 plan?

The minimum contribution for each certificate owner is $500 in total purchases within the first two years after the initial purchase. The maximum contribution is $171,500 per beneficiary. This, by the way, is an amount equal to five years' tuition and mandatory student fees at the most expensive member college. The Independent 529 plan also has an automatic purchase plan, where you can purchase a certificate for as little as $25 per month.

Does this Independent 529 plan offer the same federal tax benefits as the state-sponsored 529 plans or other 529 prepaid tuition plans?

Yes, they essentially work the same in every way except how they go about funding the tuition. Independent 529 plans offer the same federal tax benefits as state-sponsored 529 plans or other 529 prepaid tuition plans.

Are there any fees associated with the Independent 529 plan?

One of the reasons I really like the Independent 529 plan is that there are absolutely no sales, application, or maintenance fees.

Can I get a refund if a beneficiary does not attend a member college?

Yes. You can request a refund if your beneficiary does not attend a participating college. In addition, if your beneficiary attends a member college, you can also request a refund to pay for other educational expenses besides tuition and mandatory fees.

How does a refund work?

A purchaser may request a refund at any time after the one-year anniversary date of purchase. The certificate's refund value is adjusted by the actual investment return it has earned with a maximum annualized growth rate of 2 percent and a maximum annualized loss of 2 percent.

Are there any penalties if a beneficiary attends a public college?

No, there are no penalties as long as the beneficiary uses the funds for qualified higher-education expenses at an accredited college or university, public or private. If funds are not used for qualified higher-education expenses, they are subject to income tax and a 10 percent federal penalty.

Does the Independent 529 plan affect eligibility for financial aid?

The answer is possibly. Financial aid rules are constantly changing, and they vary, depending on policies of an individual institution. As of now, though, Congress has passed a new law that significantly improves the financial aid rules governing prepaid 529 plans. They're now treated as a parental asset, not a student's, so no more than 5.6 percent of your 529 plan's assets will be used to assess need when you apply for financial aid.

What if my child gets a full or partial scholarship?

It depends on what the scholarship covers. If the scholarship covers the cost of qualified expenses, you can withdraw the funds up to the amount of the scholarship without incurring the 10 percent federal tax penalty, but earnings are still subject to income tax.

What if the beneficiary or certificate owner dies before a certificate is redeemed?

If the designated beneficiary dies before the certificate is redeemed, the owner may change the beneficiary to a family member of the deceased beneficiary, or may request a refund. The 12-month holding period for refunds is waived if the beneficiary dies. A contingent certificate owner is named when an account is opened. The contingent certificate owner assumes ownership of the account upon death of the original certificate owner.

What if I do not have the full tuition amount saved in my Independent 529 account?

If the value of your certificate is less than the full amount of tuition and mandatory fees, you will be responsible for the difference at the current rate.

What if I have purchased more than the full tuition amount? What do I do?

If the value of your certificate is more than the full amount of tuition and mandatory fees, you have several options. You can: (1) save the excess for a subsequent year; (2) transfer the benefits to another family member; or (3) request a refund. Keep in mind that if the refund is not used for other qualified educational expenses, it is subject to a 10 percent federal penalty in addition to regular income tax.

What happens if the private college I'm interested in attending ends its Independent 529 plan membership?

The college will be obligated to honor all certificates that were purchased prior to its withdrawal.

Where can I find more information about this program?
Go to *www.independent529plan.com*. The site offers detailed information on the plans and lists all the participating colleges.

SECTION 529 SAVINGS PLANS

What is a Section 529 savings plan?
A Section 529 savings plan is a state-run, tax-deferred savings plan that allows you to set money aside for your child's education. Basically, a Section 529 plan is an investment program. Unlike prepaid tuition programs (see page 125), these plans do not lock in future tuition costs at today's prices. Instead, they let you invest in a tax-advantaged way against the rising costs of education. Section 529 plans carry fewer restrictions than prepaid tuition plans do, especially as to your choice of college or university.

Should I choose a 529 prepaid plan or a 529 savings plan to fund my child's education?
It depends on what type of risks you are willing to take with your money. With a prepaid plan, it is just that—prepaid—and you do not have to worry about the ups and downs of the market. With a savings plan you would have more money for college, but you could also have less than you put in; it all depends on which investment choices you make for your money within the savings plan and how they perform.

What are the main differences between a prepaid plan and a savings plan?
Many prepaid programs have a specific enrollment period each year. Prepayment contracts must be purchased during the

enrollment period, and the price of the contract is adjusted each year when the new enrollment period begins. Savings programs do not have restricted enrollment periods and accept new accounts and contributions at any time.

Almost all state-sponsored prepaid programs require that either the account owner or the beneficiary meet state residency requirements. The vast majority of savings programs, however, are open to residents of any state.

Most prepayment contracts are of limited duration. For example, the program may specify that the contract will be terminated, and a refund made, if the benefits are not used within ten years after the beneficiary's normal college matriculation date. Most savings programs, however, have no program-imposed limit on account duration, and can remain open indefinitely as long as there is a designated beneficiary on the account.

Most contract-type and voucher-type prepaid programs provide only for undergraduate tuition and fees, while savings programs can generally be used for any costs that meet the definition of "qualified higher-education expenses," including graduate school.

Do all 50 states have 529 plans?

All 50 states, and the District of Columbia, now operate 529 plans. Some states have more than one. Most of these programs are open for you to participate in even if you live in another state. A great summary of the different plans offered in each state is available through Joseph Hurley's website, *www.savingforcollege.com,* and in his invaluable book, *The Best Way to Save for College—A Complete Guide to 529 Plans.*

How much can I contribute to and/or accumulate in a 529 plan?

As of the writing of this book, around $250,000 can be contributed to 529 plan accounts for a single beneficiary. A 529 plan imposes no income limitations. Your contributions to a 529 account come out of your taxable estate. To avoid a gift tax, the best plan may be to fund your 529 at just $12,000 per year per donor, or use the IRS-approved five-year averaging method, which allows you to contribute $60,000 in a lump sum for single individuals or $120,000 for married couples (assuming you make no other gifts to that beneficiary during that five-year period).

Can a person other than a parent put money into a 529 plan?

Yes. Anyone can put money into a 529 plan, regardless of his or her relationship to the child. And, by the way, if you're thinking about going back to college, you can contribute to a 529 plan for yourself and reap the tax benefits.

What are the tax benefits of 529 plans?

They are considerable. All money taken out of a 529 plan is exempt from federal taxes if used to pay higher-education expenses. The 2006 Pension Protection Act made this federal tax-free treatment permanent for 529 withdrawals used for college.

There may also be state tax advantages. Many states follow federal income-tax treatment in excluding the earnings in your 529 accounts from state and local income taxes, and several offer a deduction for all or part of your contributions into their programs. A few states also provide other financial benefits to program participants, such as scholarships, matching contributions, or favorable state-aid treatment.

With the current capital-gains tax and dividend tax being so low, does it make more sense to invest in stocks that pay dividends or a 529 plan?

The President's package reduces taxes on dividends and capital gains but does not eliminate them. The experts still like 529s because zero tax is better than some tax. Qualified distributions from 529 plans remain tax-free. The rate is now set at 15 percent on dividends, and on capital gains. Individuals in the two lowest tax brackets (including many children) pay at a 5 percent rate through 2007 and at a zero percent rate in 2008. Also, interest income and short-term capital gains coming from taxable investments are still treated as ordinary income and taxed at rates as high as 35 percent. In many 529 plans you can find investments offering the protection of principal and competitive interest rates, without incurring the tax. The tax cuts in effect now may slightly dim the sparkle of 529 plans, but because of their multiple benefits, 529s will remain attractive and important to many investors.

Why should I invest in a 529 plan when I can't be sure that my child will attend a public university in my state?

There's a misconception that 529 plans are only geared to families that send their children to a state school. That's just not true. The states offering prepaid tuition contracts covering in-state tuition will allow you to transfer the value of your contract to private and out-of-state schools (although you may not get full value, depending on the particular state). If you decide to use a 529 savings program, the full value of your account can be used at any accredited college or university in the country (along with some foreign institutions).

How do I transfer my account from one state's 529 plan to another state's 529 plan?

A transfer of assets from one state's plan to another for the same beneficiary is a qualifying rollover, but this type of rollover can be done only once every 12 months. However, there is no limit on the frequency of rollovers where the beneficiary is replaced with a qualifying member of the family. A rollover can be transacted either through a direct "trustee-to-trustee" transfer (program permitting), or by a withdrawal of funds followed by the contribution of equivalent funds within 60 days to a different 529 plan.

A qualifying rollover will not be treated as a distribution for federal income tax. Be sure to find out how the 529 plan you are investigating handles rollover requests, as there may be restrictions imposed by the program.

Is it wise to invest in a 529 plan out of state that's been getting better returns than my state's 529 plan?

It depends on your goals, your tax bracket, and how much better the out-of-state fund is doing. Will your child want to go to an in-state college? If so, take into consideration the fact that your child won't have to pay state income taxes on the funds he or she withdraws for college expenses. Also take into account how much you will benefit from the state deductions, if any, on your contributions. Compare those bottom-line numbers with the return on the out-of-state Section 529 plan you are considering. The numbers will tell you which way to go.

My child is a senior in high school. Is it too late for me to start using a 529 plan?

Not necessarily. Assess your potential for tax savings by looking at your most recently filed tax return. Did you pay any tax on interest, dividends, or capital-gains distributions? If you did, a 529 plan represents an opportunity to convert taxable investment income into tax-free investment income. Even if an account has a life of only a few years—remember that it will usually take two to five years to earn a degree—you will be saving taxes. In fact, many parents facing college bills in the near future want to have their money in safe, interest-paying investments. This is where the tax protection of a 529 plan provides the greatest advantage.

It gets even better if you live in a state that offers a tax deduction for contributions to the home-state 529 plan. Instead of paying college bills out-of-pocket, you can reap the benefit of a state income-tax deduction by first making a contribution to the 529 plan, and then using your account to pay the bills. Bottom line: College expenses become a write-off for state income-tax purposes.

If I have a 529 savings plan for my child, will it affect his or her financial aid eligibility?

Generally speaking, the money you put *into* your 529 plan should not hurt your kid's chances for federal financial aid. According to the U.S. Department of Education (DOE), the balance in a 529 savings plan is an asset belonging to the parent or other account owner. This is the good news, because a parent's assets are "assessed" in the aid eligibility formula at no more than 5.6 percent, compared to 35 percent for investments owned by the student. And 529 plans owned by grandparents are not factored into the equation at all.

That being said, please keep in mind that schools don't necessarily follow the federal-aid formula when doling out their own scholarship funds. I am hearing that many families feel that financial aid offices are punishing them if they have assets in 529 plans, by reducing or denying their own aid awards. The most frustrating part of all of this is that there are no regulations or guidelines that all schools must follow in regard to 529 plans.

In the meantime, if you have a 529 savings plan and are

concerned about its future impact on your kid's aid eligibility, consider spending the 529 assets on college expenses as quickly as possible so the account does not impact next year's award. It might also help to switch the beneficiary designation away from the college student, either to a younger child or to you. You could also think about revoking the 529 funds, as long as the resulting tax and penalties are not too severe.

Can I change the beneficiary of my 529 account?

Yes, as long as the new beneficiary is a family member who has one of the following relationships to the current beneficiary: a son or daughter (natural or legally adopted); a stepson or step-daughter; a brother, sister, stepbrother, or stepsister; a father or mother; a stepfather or stepmother; a niece or nephew; an aunt or uncle; a son-in-law, daughter-in-law, father-in-law, mother-in-law, brother-in-law, or sister-in-law; the spouse of the desig-nated beneficiary (who must have the same principal place of abode) or the spouse of any of the relatives listed above (who must have the same principal place of abode); or a first cousin. All 529 plans accommodate a change in the beneficiary with-out imposing a penalty, although some may have age or resi-dency restrictions, and some may charge a fee. There are no federal income-tax consequences of a beneficiary change; how-ever, there can be gift-tax consequences when the new benefi-ciary is at least one generation below the old beneficiary.

Can I claim the Hope Scholarship or Lifetime Learning Credit in the same year that I withdraw from my 529 account to pay for college?

Yes. The Hope Scholarship or Lifetime Learning Credit can be claimed regardless of whether funds used for qualified tuition and related expenses come from a 529 account. However, in order to prevent "double-dipping," Section 529 requires that qualified higher-education expenses be reduced by any expenses used to determine the Hope Scholarship or Lifetime Learning Credit.

Can I transfer my child's existing UGMA/UTMA assets into a 529 plan?

Yes. If you are custodian, you can liquidate the current investments and reinvest the proceeds in a 529 plan. The sale of investments may generate a tax on capital gains. It is your responsibility as a custodian to comply with state law in handling UGMA/UTMA funds. Some parents will be disappointed to learn that a transfer of assets to a 529 plan will not result in a transfer of ownership rights from the minor to the parent. The minor will assume direct ownership of the 529 account at the age of 18 or 21, as determined by state law. For this reason, consider spending down current UGMA/UTMA assets for the benefit of the minor, and replacing those funds by contributing your own money into a 529 plan.

How do I sign up for a 529 plan?

Most 529 plans require you to complete a simple enrollment form. After that, you can make your contributions by check or credit card, or sign up for regular automatic withdrawals from a bank account.

Who decides how the money in a 529 plan is invested?

The state that manages the plan you are contributing to picks the investments or hires an investment adviser to pick the investments. This is a factor you should consider when choosing a plan. Once you've started to contribute to a plan, the state—or the investment company acting as the state's agent—takes full control of how the money is invested. In most 529 plans, the assets are allocated, according to the beneficiary's age, among stocks, bonds, and money-market funds. The younger the child, the more risk that can be taken, according to the state laws. However, some plans are far more risk-averse and conservative than others, so investigate who is managing the plan, and where your contribution will be invested. Also remember that if you choose a plan outside your state, you may forfeit a state-tax deduction. In any case, please continue to monitor the investment performance of your plan to make sure it is doing what you want.

How do I tell which plans currently are rated best overall?

On Joseph Hurley's website, *www.savingforcollege.com*, in the 5-Cap Ratings section, Joe has assigned an overall rating to each state-sponsored program, ranging from one cap (least attractive) to five caps (most attractive). In my opinion, Joe Hurley is the top expert on these plans in the United States.

What happens if my child decides not to go to college?

If your child decides not to go to college, you can use the money in the Section 529 plan to pay for another "member of the family's" education by rolling over your balance to the new family member 529 account. Or you may request a refund. This refund is known as a nonqualified distribution and will be taxed to the owner of the account. Your original contributions or deposits will be refunded to you without taxes, but your earnings will be taxed as ordinary income. You will also pay a 10 percent penalty on the earnings, but not the original contributions, which are returned. Also, if you took a state-tax deduction on your state income taxes, you will have to repay that to the state.

What happens to the money in the plan if my child dies or becomes disabled?
The penalty is usually waived.

I received a number of offers from different companies stating that if I use their credit card or register the credit cards I currently use with their program, they will contribute a percentage of the money I spend to the 529 plan of my choice. There are so many offers to choose from; do you have any recommendations?
Customer loyalty programs are a great way to get free money for college—companies give you money back for college as a way to earn your loyalty. Some of the popular college savings "accelerators" that I like are:

Upromise (www.upromise.com). Offers variable rebates from thousands of participating merchants; simply register your credit cards to get a percentage of your spending back into your Upromise Account. If you get the Citi Upromise credit card, you get another 1 percent on your eligible purchases.

BabyMint (www.babymint.com). Offers variable rebates from participating merchants when you simply register your credit cards to get a percentage of your spending. If you get the BabyMint College Savings Credit Card, you earn a 1 percent rebate on every purchase, and if you use the card at one of the participating in-store merchants, you get up to an additional 8 percent rebate on all of your purchases. BabyMint also has a Tuition Rewards program where the shopping rebates you earn are matched by tuition credits when your child chooses to attend any of the 150 participating colleges or universities. If your child chooses to attend a school that is not in the network, you can still use your BabyMint merchant rebate, but you won't qualify for any Tuition Rewards.

Fidelity 529 College Rewards MasterCard (www.fidelity.com).

Earn 2 percent rebate on eligible retail purchases, when transferred into your account with any Fidelity-managed 529. The maximum number of rewards points you can earn each year is $1,500. To apply, call (800) 551-0839, or apply online.

FINANCIAL AID: THE BASICS

Who awards financial aid, and what forms does it take?

Most financial aid comes from the federal Department of Education (*www.ed.gov*). Federal student aid can take many forms. Those forms include grants, work-study programs, and loans. Grants are outright gifts for educational purposes; you don't have to pay them back. Work-study programs allow you to earn money for your education while attending school. Loans let you borrow money, often at a favorable rate, to pay educational expenses. In addition to aid that is provided by the federal government, you can also learn about state programs by contacting your state Department of Education.

How do grants differ from scholarships? Are they better in the long run?

Grants are the best kind of aid there is. Unlike scholarships, grants can't be rescinded if a student fails to maintain his grade point average or athletic commitments. Like scholarships, grants do not have to be repaid.

What are some of the best undergraduate grants to pursue, and how much help will I get if I qualify?

The Pell Grant is the best-known federal grant for undergraduate students, and in 2006–2007 the maximum amount awarded was $4,050 for the year. Another federal grant, the Supplemental Educational Opportunity Grant (SEOG), is available to undergraduates with "exceptional" financial need—those whose families can contribute very little to the cost of college. Even so, the largest SEOG grant you can receive is $4,000 per year. By all means, try to get one or both of these, but don't count on grants to get you through four years of college.

How does a scholarship differ from a grant?

Hundreds of thousands of scholarships and fellowships from several thousand institutional and private sponsors are awarded each year. Generally, scholarships and fellowships are reserved for students with special talents, whether those talents are academic, athletic, or artistic. Associations organized by ethnicity, sex, and religion, promoting certain fields of study, or even geographic regions of the country also offer scholarships to students. Basically, if you look hard enough, you can find at least several scholarships for which you qualify to apply. Unlike loans, scholarships do not have to be repaid, but they may be rescinded.

Where can I get information about private grants and scholarships?

There are some excellent sources of information on the Internet. Check out *www.fastweb.com,* a scholarship search engine that lets Internet users search, without cost, a database of more than 180,000 scholarships. Also see the U.S. Department of Education's website, *www.ed.gov.*

As a parent, can I take out a federal loan?

It's the student who typically applies for and receives a federally guaranteed loan. Loans have become a major part of many

FINANCIAL AID: THE BASICS

students' financial-aid packages. They often come at very low interest rates—as low as 5 percent.

One loan that students are likely to be eligible for is a federally granted student loan. In addition to carrying a low interest rate, this loan does not require credit checks or collateral. The repayment terms are liberal, and deferment options are numerous and flexible. If a student or parent has to borrow additional money, a local bank, credit union, or college might also make a loan.

What other kinds of aid are available?

The Federal Work-Study Program is one common form of supplemental financial aid that many students qualify for. Those who qualify work part-time in a university department or office that is, whenever possible, related to the student's field of study.

When looking for a school that will give me financial aid, I was told to look for one with a large endowment fund. Why?

Schools with large endowment funds can afford to be more generous with financial aid. Such schools tend to define "need" liberally, particularly when the student is talented. For you, this means a better chance of receiving a scholarship or an aid package.

Can I apply for financial aid before my child is even accepted at a college?

In the case of federal financial aid, the answer is yes, and the sooner you apply the better, because the money is awarded to applicants on a first-come, first-served basis. Starting in January of the year in which your child will enter college, you should fill out a Free Application for Federal Student Aid (FAFSA), the form the government uses to determine how much federal aid you qualify for based on your income and that of the child attending college. You can find the form on the Internet site *www.ed.gov*, or you can request a FAFSA from your child's high school, any college, or the Federal Student Aid Information Center, P.O. Box 84, Washington, D.C. 20044; (800) 433-3243.

Do college financial-aid applications require both parents to list income and assets? I am divorced and solely responsible for my children's education, but I'm afraid my children won't qualify for financial aid if their father's income is considered.

Twenty-seven percent of all financial-aid applicants come from divorced families, so this is a common problem. Financial aid is complicated enough, and divorce makes it more so. Colleges want to know about the finances of both parents, and remarried parents must also provide financial information about their new spouses. Most colleges consider each student's individual situation and make case-by-case decisions.

Should I use a financial adviser to plan for my children's college education?

You can and should do a lot of research and thinking about your family's needs on your own, but you can also benefit greatly from talking to a financial adviser who is familiar with recent developments in this area of financial planning. *Saving-forcollege.com* posts a directory of advisers who know the ins and outs of 529 plans. The National Institute of Certified College Planning Specialists (*www.niccp.com*) trains financial professionals in the art of college financial planning and can refer you to capable advisers nationwide.

ADDITIONAL RESOURCES

RETIREMENT RESOURCES

SOCIAL SECURITY

To get a Social Security estimate, call toll-free (800) 772-1213. You can also contact the Social Security Administration on line at *www.ssa.gov.*

Call your local Social Security office and ask for any of the following publications:

How Your Retirement Benefit Is Figured (Publication 05-10070)
Understanding Social Security (Publication 05-10024)
The Appeals Process (Publication 05-10141)
Retirement Benefits (Publication 05-10035)
When You Get Social Security Resources or Survivor Benefits: What You Need to Know (Publication 05-10077)

AARP has a number of useful publications that can be found on their website. Also, *www.aarp.org/socialsecurity/* has a wealth of information about Social Security.

AARP
601 E Street NW
Washington, DC 20049
(888) 687-2277
www.aarp.org

PENSIONS

Pension Benefit Guaranty Corporation (PBGC) is a federal agency that protects employer-sponsored defined-benefit plans. The PBGC invites people to call their customer service representatives for assistance at (202) 326-4000. You can also visit their website at *www.pbgc.gov*.

The Employee Retirement Income Security Act of 1974 (ERISA) is a federal law that sets minimum standards for pension plans in private industry, including 401(k)s. The U.S. Department of Labor is the agency that oversees these standards.

For information about pensions, call the Department of Labor's Employee Benefits Security Administration toll-free at (866) 487-2365, or check out their website: *www.dol.gov/ebsa*. You can direct questions about your pension plan to your state labor office.

STATE LABOR OFFICES

Alabama

Commissioner
Alabama Department of Labor
P.O. Box 303500
Montgomery, AL 36130-3500
Phone: 334-242-3460
Fax: 334-240-3417

Director
Department of Industrial Relations
Industrial Relations Building
649 Monroe Street, Room 204
Montgomery, AL 36131
Phone: 334-242-8990
Fax: 334-242-3960
www.dir.state.al.us

Alaska

Commissioner
Department of Labor and Workforce Development
P.O. Box 21149
Juneau, AK 99801-1149
Phone: 907-465-2700
Fax: 907-465-2784
www.labor.state.ak.us

Arizona

Chairman
Industrial Commission
P.O. Box 19070
Phoenix, AZ 85005-9070
Phone: 602-542-4411
Fax: 602-542-7889

Director
State Labor Department
P.O. Box 19070
Phoenix, AZ 85005-9070

Phone: 602-542-4515
Fax: 602-542-8097
www.ica.state.az.us

Arkansas

Director
Department of Labor
10421 West Markham
Little Rock, AR 72205
Phone: 501-682-4541
Fax: 501-682-4535
www.state.ar.us/labor

California

Director
Department of Industrial Relations
455 Golden Gate Avenue, 10th Floor
San Francisco, CA 94102
Phone: 415-703-5050
Fax: 415-703-5059

State Labor Commissioner
Division of Labor Standards Enforcement
Department of Industrial Relations
455 Golden Gate Avenue, 9th Floor
San Francisco, CA 94102
Phone: 415-703-4810
Fax: 415-703-4807
www.dir.ca.gov

Colorado

Executive Director
Department of Labor and Employment
633 17th Street, Second Floor
Denver, CO 80202-3660
Phone: 303-318-8000
Fax: 303-318-8048

Director
Division of Labor
633 17th Street, Suite 200
Denver, CO 80202-3660
Phone: 303-318-8441
Fax: 303-318-8400
www.coworkforce.com/lab

Connecticut

Commissioner
Labor Department
200 Folly Brook Boulevard
Wethersfield, CT 06109-1114
Phone: 860-263-6505
Fax: 860-263-6529
www.ctdol.state.ct.us

Delaware

Secretary
Department of Labor
4425 North Market Street, 4th Floor
Wilmington, DE 19802
Phone: 302-761-8000
Fax: 302-761-6621
www.delawareworks.com

District of Columbia

Director
Department of Employment Services
Employment Security Building
54 New York Avenue NE, Suite 3007
Washington, D.C. 20002
Phone: 202-671-1900
Fax: 202-673-6993
www.does.ci.washington.dc.us

ADDITIONAL RESOURCES

Florida

Secretary
Department of Business and Professional Regulation
1940 North Monroe Street
Tallahassee, FL 32399-0750
Phone: 850-488-3131
Fax: 850-487-1044
www.state.fl.us/dbpr/ or *www.MyFlorida.com*
(Farm labor and child labor)

Director
Agency for Workforce Innovation
Caldwell Building, Suite 100
107 East Madison Street
Tallahassee, FL 32399-4120
Phone: 850-245-7105
Fax: 850-921-3223
www.floridajobs.org/ or *www.MyFlorida.com*
(Employment related services)

Georgia

Commissioner
Department of Labor
Sussex Place, Room 600
148 International Blvd., NE
Atlanta, GA 30303
Phone: 404-656-3011
Fax: 404-656-2683
www.dol.state.ga.us

Guam

Director
Department of Labor
Government of Guam
P.O. Box 9970
Tamuning, GU 96931-9970
Phone: 671-647-6510/12
Fax: 671-647-6517
www.guamdol.net

Hawaii

Director
Department of Labor and Industrial Relations
830 Punchbowl Street, Room 321
Honolulu, HI 96813
Phone: 808-586-8865/8844
Fax: 808-586-9099
www.hawaii.gov/labor

Idaho

Director
Department of Labor
317 West Main Street
Boise, ID 83735-0001
Phone: 208-332-3579
Fax: 208-334-6430
www.labor.state.id.us

Illinois

Director
Department of Labor
160 North LaSalle Street, 13th Floor, Suite C-1300
Chicago, IL 60601
Phone: 312-793-1808
Fax: 312-793-5257
www.state.il.us/agency/idol

Indiana

Commissioner
Department of Labor
Indiana Government Center South
402 West Washington Street, Room W195
Indianapolis, IN 46204-2739
Phone: 317-232-2378
Fax: 317-233-5381
www.state.in.us/labor or *www.in.gov/labor/childlabor/safety.html*

Iowa

Director
Iowa Workforce Development
1000 East Grand Avenue
Des Moines, IA 50319-0209
Phone: 515-281-5365
Fax: 515-281-4698

Labor Commissioner
Division of Labor Services
1000 East Grand Avenue
Des Moines, IA 50319
Phone: 515-281-3447
Fax: 515-281-4698
www.iowaworkforce.org/labor

Kansas

Secretary
Department of Human Resources
401 Southwest Topeka Boulevard
Topeka, KS 66603-3182
Phone: 785-296-7474
Fax: 785-368-6294
www.dol.ks.gov

Kentucky

Commissioner
Kentucky Department of Labor
1047 U.S. Highway 127 South, Suite 4
Frankfort, KY 40601-4381
Phone: 502-564-3070
Fax: 502-564-5387
www.labor.ky.gov

Louisiana

Secretary
Department of Labor
P.O. Box 94094
Baton Rouge, LA 70804-9094
Phone: 225-342-3011
Fax: 225-342-3778
www.ldol.state.la.us

Maine

Commissioner
Department of Labor
19 Union Street
P.O. Box 259
Augusta, ME 04332-0259
Phone: 207-287-3787
Fax: 207-287-5292

Director
Bureau of Labor Standards
Department of Labor
State House Station #45
Augusta, ME 04333-0045
Phone: 207-624-6400
Fax: 207-624-6449
www.state.me.us/labor

Maryland

Secretary
Department of Labor, Licensing and Regulation
500 North Calvert Street, Suite 401
Baltimore, MD 21202
Phone: 410-230-6020 ext. 1393
Fax: 410-333-0853

Assistant Secretary
Department of Labor, Division of Workforce Development
1100 Eutaw Street, 6th Floor
Baltimore, MD 21201
Phone: 410-767-2999
Fax: 410-767-2986
www.dllr.state.md.us

Massachusetts

Director
Department of Labor & Work Force Development
1 Ashburton Place, Room 2112
Boston, MA 02108
Phone: 617-727-6573
Fax: 617-727-1090
www.mass.gov/dlwd or *www.state.ma.us*

Michigan

Director
Department of Labor and Economic Growth
P.O. Box 30004
Lansing, MI 48909
Phone: 517-373-3034
Fax: 517-373-2129
www.michigan.gov/cis

Minnesota

Commissioner
Department of Labor and Industry
443 Lafayette Road
St. Paul, MN 55155
Phone: 651-284-5010
Fax: 651-284-5721
www.doli.state.mn.us

Mississippi

Executive Director
Mississippi Department of Employment Security
P.O. Box 1699
Jackson, MS 39215-1699
Phone: 601-321-6100
Fax: 601-321-6104
www.mississippi.gov

Missouri

Chairman
Labor and Industrial Relations Commission
P.O. Box 599
3315 West Truman Boulevard
Jefferson City, MO 65102-0599
Phone: 573-751-2461
Fax: 573-751-7806

Members of the Commission
Labor and Industrial Relations Commission
P.O. Box 599
Jefferson City, MO 65102-0599
Phone: 573-751-2461
Fax: 573-751-7806

Director
Department of Labor & Industrial Relations
P.O. Box 504
Jefferson City, MO 65102-0504
Phone: 573-751-9691
Fax: 573-751-4135
www.dolir.mo.gov

Montana

Commissioner
Department of Labor and Industry
P.O. Box 1728
Helena, MT 59624-1728
Phone: 406-444-9091
Fax: 406-444-1394
www.dli.state.mt.us

Nebraska

Commissioner
Department of Labor
550 South 16th Street
Box 94600
Lincoln, NE 68509-4600
Phone: 402-471-3405
Fax: 402-471-2318
www.dol.state.ne.us

Nevada

Commissioner
Office of the Nevada Labor Commissioner
Department of Business and Industry
555 East Washington Avenue, Suite 4100
Las Vegas, NV 89101-1050
Phone: 702-486-2650
Fax: 702-486-2660
www.LaborCommissioner.com or *www.dbi.state.nv.us*

New Hampshire

Commissioner
Department of Labor
95 Pleasant Street
Concord, NH 03301
Phone: 603-271-3171
Fax: 603-271-6852
www.labor.state.nh.us

New Jersey

Commissioner
New Jersey Department of Labor
John Fitch Plaza
13th Floor, Suite D
P.O. Box 110
Trenton, NJ 08625-0110
Phone: 609-292-2323
Fax: 609-633-9271
www.state.nj.us/labor/index.html

New Mexico

Secretary
Department of Labor
P.O. Box 1928
401 Broadway, NE
Albuquerque, NM 87103-1928
Phone: 505-841-8409
Fax: 505-841-8491
www.dol.state.nm.us

New York

Commissioner
Department of Labor
State Campus, Building 12, Room 500
Albany, NY 12240-0003
Phone: 518-457-2741
Fax: 518-457-6908
or
345 Hudson Street
New York, NY 10014-0675
Phone: 212-352-6000
www.labor.state.ny.us

North Carolina

Commissioner
Department of Labor
4 West Edenton Street
Raleigh, NC 27601-1092
Phone: 919-733-0359
Fax: 919-733-0223
www.nclabor.com

North Dakota

Commissioner
Department of Labor
State Capitol Building
600 East Boulevard, Department 406
Bismark, ND 58505-0340
Phone: 701-328-2660
Fax: 701-328-2031
www.state.nd.us/labor

Ohio

Director
Department of Commerce
77 South High Street, 23rd Floor
Columbus, OH 43215
Phone: 614-644-7047
Fax: 614-644-8292

Superintendant
Division of Labor and Worker Safety
50 West Broad Street, 28th Floor
Columbus, OH 43215
Phone: 614-644-2239
Fax: 614-728-8639/5650
www.ohio.gov/contacts.stm

Ohio Department of Job & Family Services
Office of Unemployment Compensation Deputy Director
4300 Kimberly Parkway, 4th Floor
Columbus, OH 43232
Phone: 614-995-7066
Fax: 614-466-6873
www.jfs.ohio.gov/ouc

Oklahoma

Commissioner
Department of Labor
4001 North Lincoln Boulevard
Oklahoma City, OK 73105-5212
Phone: 405-528-1500, ext. 200
Fax: 405-528-5751
www.state.ok.us/~okdol

Oregon

Commissioner
Bureau of Labor and Industries
800 NE Oregon Street #32
Portland, OR 97232
Phone: 503-731-4070
Fax: 503-731-4103
www.boli.state.or.us

Pennsylvania

Secretary
Department of Labor and Industry
1700 Labor and Industry Building
7th and Forster Streets
Harrisburg, PA 17120
Phone: 717-787-5279
Fax: 717-787-8826
www.dli.state.pa.us

Puerto Rico

Secretary
Department of Labor & Human Resources
Edificio Prudencio Rivera Martinez
505 Munoz Rivera Avenue
G.P.O. Box 3088
Hato Rey, PR 00918
Phone: 787-754-2119 or 2120
Fax: 787-753-9550
www.osha.gov/oshdir/stateprogs/Puerto_Rico.html

Rhode Island

Director
Department of Labor and Training
1511 Pontiac Avenue
Cranston, RI 02920
Phone: 401-462-8870
Fax: 401-462-8872
www.det.state.ri.us

South Carolina

Director
Department of Labor, Licensing & Regulations
Synergy Center, Kingstree Building
110 Center View Drive
P.O. Box 11329
Columbia, SC 29211-1329
Phone: 803-896-4300
Fax: 803-896-4393
www.llr.state.sc.us

South Dakota

Secretary
Department of Labor
700 Governors Drive
Pierre, SD 57501-2291
Phone: 605-773-3101
Fax: 605-773-4211
www.state.sd.us/dol/dol.htm

Tennessee

Commissioner
Department of Labor
Andrew Johnson Tower
710 James Robertson Parkway, 8th Floor
Nashville, TN 37243-0655
Phone: 615-741-6642
Fax: 615-741-5078
www.state.tn.us/labor-wfd

Texas

Executive Director
Texas Workforce Commission
101 East 15th Street, Room 618
Austin, TX 78778
Phone: 512-463-0735
Fax: 512-475-2321

Commissioner Representing Labor
Texas Workforce Commission
101 East 15th Street, Room 674
Austin, TX 78778
Phone: 512-463-2829
Fax: 512-475-2152
www.twc.state.tx.us

Utah

Commissioner
Utah Labor Commission
P.O. Box 146610
Salt Lake City, UT 84114-6610
Phone: 801-530-6880
Fax: 801-530-6804
www.labor.state.ut.us

Vermont

Commissioner
Vermont Department of Labor
5 Green Mountain Drive
P.O. Box 488
Montpelier, VT 05602-0488
Phone: 802-828-4000
Fax: 802-828-4022
www.labor.vermont.gov

Virgin Islands

Commissioner of Labor
Department of Labor
2203 Church Street
St. Croix, U.S. VI 00802-4612
Phone: 340-776-3700
Fax: 340-773-0094
www.vidol.gov

Commissioner of Labor
Department of Labor
P. O. Box 302608
St. Thomas, U.S. VI 00803-2608
Phone: 340-776-3700, 340-774-5908
Fax: 340-774-5908
www.vidol.gov

Virginia

Commissioner
Department of Labor and Industry
Powers-Taylor Building
13 South 13th Street
Richmond, VA 23219
Phone: 804-786-2377
Fax: 804-371-6524
www.dli.state.va.us

Washington

Director
Department of Labor & Industries
P.O. Box 44001
Olympia, WA 98504-4001
Phone: 360-902-4203
Fax: 360-902-4202
www.lni.wa.gov

West Virginia

Commissioner
Division of Labor
Bureau of Commerce
State Capitol Complex
Building #6, Room B749
Charleston, WV 25305
Phone: 304-558-7890
Fax: 304-558-3797
www.labor.state.wv.us

Wisconsin

Secretary
Department of Workforce Development
201 East Washington Avenue, #A400
P.O. Box 7946
Madison, WI 53707-7946
Phone: 608-267-9692
Fax: 608-266-1784
www.dwd.state.wi.us

Wyoming

Director
Department of Employment
1510 East Pershing Boulevard
Cheyenne, WY 82002
Phone: 307-777-7672
Fax: 307-777-5805

Program Manager
Labor Standards
Department of Employment
1510 East Pershing Boulevard
West Wing
Cheyenne, WY 82002
Phone: 307-777-7261
Fax: 307-777-5633
http://wydoe.state.wy.us/

ADDITIONAL RESOURCES

You can request a copy of the Department of Labor's *Protect Your Pension: A Quick Reference Guide* by writing to:

U.S. Department of Labor
Pension and Welfare Benefits Administration
Washington, DC 20210
(866) 4-USADOL
www.dol.gov

Another useful publication, *Your Pension: Things You Should Know About Your Pension Plan,* is available from:

Pension Benefit Guarantee Corp.
2020 K Street NW
Washington, DC 20006
(202) 326-4000
www.pbgc.gov

Other associations and brochures to help you plan your retirement:

National Council on Aging
409 3rd Street SW
Suite 200
Washington, DC 20024
(202) 479-1200

For free IRS publications, call toll-free (800) 829-1040 or visit *www.irs.gov*. Ask for *Individual Retirement Arrangements* (Publication 590).

FINANCIAL AID RESOURCES

ONLINE INFORMATION

On *www.finaid.org* you will find everything you need, including calculators to help you do the math on loan payments, college cost projections, financial-aid estimation forms, reference book resources, videotape resources, information on free booklets by mail, periodicals, lobbying and advocacy groups, and discussion groups.

A great website for information about financial aid with all the latest information about state and federal plans is run by Joseph Hurley at *www.savingforcollege.com*. Hurley has also written a terrific book on the subject, *The Best Way to Save for College*.

Another useful site is *www.collegesavings.org*.

FEDERAL STUDENT AID (FAFSA)

The Free Application for Federal Student Aid (FAFSA) is used to apply for most state loan, grant, and scholarship programs, in addition to the federal loans and grants. When you submit the FAFSA to the U.S. Department of Education, they forward the information on the form to the state student assistance agency. You must submit the FAFSA every year that you want to receive aid. The FAFSA is available in paper and electronic formats. You can get the paper version from your high school, the financial-aid office at any college or university, the public library, or by calling (800) 4-FED-AID.

If you prefer, you can fill out a Web-based version of the FAFSA at *www.fafsa.ed.gov* (step-by-step instructions are provided on this site).

Each state has a different FAFSA submission deadline. If you submit your FAFSA by March 1, you will be in time for all state deadlines, other than Michigan's. If you miss the deadline, you will be ineligible to receive state aid for the entire academic year. Procedures for applying for state prepaid tuition programs and the National Guard differ from state to state. The amount of information provided on the states' websites varies. Some states provide comprehensive information about residency requirements, loan, grant, scholarship and prepaid tuition programs, and other state aid programs. Others provide minimal information. It's a good idea to visit the sites for your state of residence and also for the states of the colleges to which you are applying.

Alabama

Alabama Commission on Higher Education
100 North Union Street
P.O. Box 302000
Montgomery, AL 36105-2310
(334) 281-1998
www.ache.state.al.us
or
Alabama State Department of Education
50 North Ripley Street
P.O. Box 302101
Montgomery, AL 36104
(334) 242-9700
www.alse.edu

Alaska

Alaska Commission on Postsecondary Education
3030 Vintage Boulevard
Juneau, AK 99801-7109
(907) 465-2967
www.state.ak.us/acpe

or
Alaska Department of Education
801 West 10th Street, Suite 200
Juneau, AK 99801-1894
(907) 465-2800
www.eed.state.ak.us

Arizona

Arizona Board of Regents
2020 North Central Avenue, Suite 230
Phoenix, AZ 85004-4593
(602) 229-2500
www.abor.asu.edu
or
Arizona Department of Education
1535 West Jefferson
Phoenix, AZ 85007
(602) 542-2147
www.ade.state.az.us

Arkansas

Arkansas Department of Higher Education
114 East Capitol
Little Rock, AR 72201-3818
(501) 371-2000
www.arkansashighered.com
or
Arkansas Department of Education
4 State Capitol Mall, Room 304A
Little Rock, AR 72201-1071
(501) 682-4474

California

California Postsecondary Education Commission
1303 J Street, Suite 500
Sacramento, CA 95814-2938
(916) 445-7933
www.cpec.ca.gov
or

California Department of Education
1430 North Street
Sacramento, CA 95814
(916) 657-2451
www.cde.ca.gov

Colorado

Colorado Commission on Higher Education
18 Lawrence Street, Suite 1200
Denver, CO 80204
(303) 866-2723
www.state.co.us/cche

or

Colorado Department of Education
201 East Colfax Avenue
Denver, CO 80203-1705
(303) 866-6600
www.cde.state.co.us

Connecticut

Connecticut Department of Higher Education
61 Woodland Street
Hartford, CT 06105-2326
(860) 947-1855
www.ctdhe.org

or

Connecticut Department of Education
165 Capitol Avenue
Hartford, CT 06145
(860) 713-6548
www.state.ct.us/sde

Delaware

Delaware Higher Education Commission
Carvel State Office Building, Fourth Floor
820 North French Street
Wilmington, DE 19801
(302) 577-3240
www.doe.state.de.us/high-ed

or

Delaware Department of Education
401 Federal Street
P.O. Box 1402
Dover, DE 19903-1402
(302) 739-4601
www.doe.state.de.us

District of Columbia

District of Columbia State Education Office
Post Secondary Financial Assistance
John A. Wilson Building
1350 Pennsylvania Avenue NW
Washington, DC 20004
(202) 727-1000
http://seo.dc.gov/services/post_secondary_ Financial_assistance/ index2.shtm

or

District of Columbia Public Schools
825 North Capitol Street NE, 7th Floor
Washington, DC 20002
(202) 724-4222
www.k12.dc.us

Florida

Florida Department of Education
Office of the Commissioner
Turlington Building, Suite 1514
325 West Gaines Street
Tallahassee, FL 32399
(850) 245-0505
www.fldoe.org

Georgia

Georgia Student Finance Commission
2082 East Exchange Place
Tucker, GA 30084
(770) 724-9000
www.gsfc.org

or
State Department of Education
2054 Twin Towers East, 205 Butler Street
Atlanta, GA 30334-5040
(404) 656-5812
www.gadoe.org

Hawaii

Hawaii State Postsecondary Education Commission
University of Hawaii, Bachman Hall
2444 Dole Street, Room 209
Honolulu, HI 96822
(808) 948-8213
www.Free-4u.com/state_postsecondary_education_commission.htm
or
Hawaii Department of Education
1390 Miller Street
Honolulu, HI 96813
(808) 733-9103
http://doe.k12.h:.us

Idaho

Idaho Board of Education
P.O. Box 83720
Boise, ID 83720-0037
(208) 334-2270
www.idahoboard.Fed.org
or
Idaho State Department of Education
650 West State Street
Boise, ID 83720-0027
(208) 332-6800
www.sde.state.id.us/Dept

Illinois

Illinois State Board of Education
100 N 1st Street
Springfield, IL 62777
(866) 262-6663
www.isbe.state.il.us

Indiana

State Student Assistance Commission of Indiana
150 West Market Street, Suite 500
Indianapolis, IN 46204
(317) 232-2350
www.in.gov/ssaci
or
Indiana Department of Education
Room 229, State House
Indianapolis, IN 46204-2798
(317) 232-6610
www.doe.state.in.us

Iowa

Iowa Department of Education
Grimes State Office Building
Des Moines, IA 50319-0146
(515) 281-5294
www.state.ia.us/educate

Kansas

Kansas Board of Regents
1000 SW Jackson Street, Suite 520
Topeka, KS 6612-1368
(785) 296-3421
www.kansas.regents.org
or
Kansas State Department of Education
120 SE 10th Avenue
Topeka, KS 66612-1182
(785) 296-3201
www.ksbe.state.ks.us

Kentucky

Kentucky Higher Education Assistance Authority
P.O. Box 798
Frankfort, KY 40602-0798
(800) 928-8926
www.kheaa.com
or

Kentucky Department of Education
500 Mero Street
Frankfort, KY 40601
(502) 564-4770
www.k12.ky.us

Louisiana

Louisiana Office of Student Financial Assistance
P.O. Box 91202
Baton Rouge, LA 70821-9202
(800) 259-5626
www.osfa.state.la.us
or
State Department of Education
P.O. Box 94064
626 North 4th Street, 12th Floor
Baton Rouge, LA 70804-9064
(877) 453-2721
www.doe.state.la.us

Maine

Finance Authority of Maine
5 Community Drive
P.O. Box 949
Augusta, ME 04332-0949
(207) 623-3263 or (800) 228-3734
www.famemaine.com
or
Maine Department of Education
23 State House Station
Augusta, ME 04333-0023
(207) 287-5800
www.state.me.us/education

Maryland

Maryland Higher Education Commission
839 Bestgate Road, Suite 400
Annapolis, Maryland 21401
(410) 260-4500
www.mhec.state.md.us

or
Maryland State Department of Education
200 West Baltimore Street
Baltimore, Maryland 21201
(410) 767-0100
www.msde.state.md.us

Massachusetts

Massachusetts Board of Higher Education
One Ashburton Place, Room 1401
Boston, MA 02108-1696
(617) 794-6950
www.mass.edu
or
Massachusetts Department of Education
350 Main Street
Malden, MA 02148-5023
(617) 388-3300
www.doe.mass.edu
or
Massachusetts Higher Education Information Center
700 Boylston Street
Boston, MA 02116
(617) 536-0200
www.heic.org

Michigan

Bureau of Student Financial Aid
Office of Information and Resources
P.O. Box 30466
Lansing, MI 48909-7966
(877) 323-2287
www.michigan.gov/mistudentaid
or
Michigan Department of Education
608 West Allegan Street
Lansing, MI 48933
(517) 373-3324
www.michigan.gov/mde

Minnesota

Minnesota Higher Education Services Office
1450 Energy Park Drive, Suite 350
St. Paul, MN 55108-5227
(651) 642-0567
www.mheso.state.mn.us
or
Minnesota Department of Education
1500 Highway 36 West
Roseville, Minnesota 55113-4266
(651) 582-8200
http://education.state.mn.us

Mississippi

Mississippi Postsecondary Education
Financial Assistance Board
3825 Ridgewood Road
Jackson, MS 39211-6453
(800) 327-2980
www.ihl.state.ms.us
or
Mississippi Department of Education
Central High School
P.O. Box 771
Jackson, MS 39205
(601) 359-3513
www.mde.k12.ms.us

Missouri

Missouri Department of Higher Education
3515 Amazonas Drive
Jefferson City, MO 65109-5717
(573) 751-2361
or

Missouri State Department of Elementary and
Secondary Education
P.O. Box 480
Jefferson City, MO 65102
(573) 751-4212
www.dese.state.mo.us

Montana

Montana University System
2500 Broadway
Helena, MT 59620-3103
(406) 444-3095
or
Montana Office of Public Instruction
P.O. Box 202501
Helena, MT 59620-2501
(406) 444-3095
www.opi.state.mt.us

Nebraska

Coordinating Commission for Postsecondary Education
P.O. Box 95005
Lincoln, NE 68509-5005
(402) 471-2847
www.ccpe.state.ne.us
or
Nebraska Department of Education
301 Centennial Mall South
Lincoln, NE 68509
(402) 471-2295
www.nde.state.ne.us

Nevada

Nevada Department of Education
700 East Fifth Street
Carson City, NV 89701
(775) 687-9200
www.nde.state.nu.us

New Hampshire
New Hampshire Postsecondary Education Commission
3 Barrell Court, Suite 300
Concord, NH 03301-8543
(603) 271-2555
www.state.nh.us/postsecondary
or
New Hampshire State Department of Education
101 Pleasant Street
Concord, NH 03301-3860
(603) 271-3494
www.ed.state.nh.us

New Jersey
State of New Jersey
Higher Education Student Assistance Authority
P.O. Box 540
Trenton, NJ 08625
(800) 792-8670
www.hessa.org
or
New Jersey Department of Education
225 West State Street
Trenton, NJ 08625-0500
(609) 292-4469
www.state.nj.us/education

New Mexico
New Mexico Commission on Higher Education
1068 Cerrillos Road
Santa Fe, NM 87505
(505) 476-6500
www.nmche.org
or
New Mexico State Department of Education
300 Don Gaspar
Santa Fe, NM 87501-2786
(505) 827-5800
www.sde.state.nm.us

New York

New York State Higher Education Services Corporation
One Commerce Plaza
Albany, NY 12255
(518) 473-1574 or (888) NYS-HESC (888-697-4372)
www.hesc.state.ny.us
or
New York State Education Department
89 Washington Avenue
Albany, NY 12234
(518) 474-5705
www.nysed.gov

North Carolina

North Carolina State Education Assistance Authority
P.O. Box 14103
Research Triangle Park, NC 27709
(919) 549-8614
www.ncesaa.edu
or
North Carolina Department of Public Instruction
301 North Wilmington Street
Raleigh, NC 27601
(919) 807-3300
www.dpi.state.nc.us

North Dakota

North Dakota Student Financial Assistance Program
Capitol Building, 10th Floor
Bismarck, ND 58505
(701) 224-4114
www.Free-4u.com/student_Financial_assistance_program.htm
or
North Dakota Department of Public Instruction
600 East Boulevard Avenue, Dept. 201
Bismarck, ND 58505-0440
(701) 328-2260
www.dpi.state.nd.us

Ohio

Ohio Board of Regents
30 East Broad Street, 36th Floor
Columbus, OH 43215-3414
(614) 466-6000
www.regents.ohio.gov
or
Ohio Department of Education
25 South Front Street
Columbus, OH 43215-4183
(877) 644-6338

Oklahoma

Oklahoma State Regents for Higher Education
655 Research Parkway, Suite 200
Oklahoma City, OK 73104
(405) 225-9100
www.okhighered.org
or
Oklahoma State Department of Education
2500 North Lincoln Boulevard
Oklahoma City, OK 73105-4599
(405) 521-3301
http://sde.state.ok.us

Oregon

Oregon State Scholarship Commission
Eugene, OR 97401
(503) 686-4166
www.Free-4u.com/oregon_state_scholarship_commission.htm
or
Oregon State Board of Higher Education
P.O. Box 3175
Eugene, OR 97403
(541) 346-5700
www.ous.edu/board
or

Oregon Department of Education
255 Capitol Street NE
Salem, OR 97310-0203
(503) 378-3569
www.ode.state.or.us

Pennsylvania

Pennsylvania Higher Education Assistance Agency
1200 North Seventh Street
Harrisburg, PA 17102-1444
(800) 692-7435
www.pheaa.org
or
Pennsylvania Department of Education
333 Market Street
Harrisburg, PA 17126
(717) 783-6788
www.pde.state.pa.us

Rhode Island

Rhode Island Board of Governors for Higher Education
50 Holden Street
Providence, RI 02908
(401) 222-2088
www.ribghe.org
or
Rhode Island Higher Education Assistance Authority
560 Jefferson Boulevard
Warwick, RI 02886
(800) 922-9855
www.riheaa.org
or
Rhode Island Department of Education
255 Westminister Street
Providence, RI 02903
(401) 222-4600
www.ridoe.net

South Carolina

South Carolina Higher Education Tuition Grants Commission
101 Business Park Boulevard, Suite 2100
Columbia, SC 29203-9498
(803) 896-1120
www.sctuitiongrants.com
or
South Carolina State Department of Education
1429 Senate Street
Columbia, SC 29201
(803) 734-8815
www.state.sde.state.sc.us

South Dakota

South Dakota Department of Education
700 Governors Drive
Pierre, SD 57501
(605) 773-3426
www.state.sd.us/deca

Tennessee

Tennessee Higher Education Commission
404 James Robertson Parkway
Suite 1900
Nashville, TN 37243
(615) 741-3605
www.state.tn.us/thec
or
Tennessee Department of Education
Andrew Johnson Tower, 6th Floor
Nashville, TN 37243-0375
(615) 741-2731
www.state.tn.us/education

Texas

Texas Education Agency
1701 North Congress Avenue
Austin, TX 78701
(512) 463-9734
www.tea.state.tx.us

Utah

Utah State Board of Regents
Board of Regents Building, The Gateway
600 South 400 West
Salt Lake City, UT 84101-1284
(801) 321-7100
www.utahsbr.edu
or
Utah State Office of Education
250 East 500 South
P.O. Box 144200
Salt Lake City, UT 84111-4200
(801) 538-7779
www.usoe.k12.ut.us

Vermont

Vermont Student Assistance Corporation
P.O. Box 2000
Champlain Mill
Winooski, VT 05404
(800) 642-3177
www.vsac.org
or
Vermont Department of Education
120 State Street
Montpelier, VT 05620-2501
(802) 828-3147
www.state.ut.us/educ

Virginia

State Council of Higher Education for Virginia
101 North Fourteenth Street
Richmond, VA 23219
(804) 225-2600
www.schev.edu
or

Virginia Department of Education
P.O. Box 2120
Richmond, VA 23218
(804) 225-2072
www.pen.k12.va.us

Washington

Washington State Higher Education Coordinating Board
Lakeridge Way
P.O. Box 43430, 917
Olympia, WA 98504-3430
(360) 753-7800
www.hecb.wa.gov
or
Washington Department of Public Instruction
Old Capitol Building, P.O. Box 47200
Olympia, WA 98504-7200
(360) 725-6000
www.k12.wa.us

West Virginia

West Virginia Department of Education
1018 Kanawha Boulevard East
Charleston, WV 25305
(304) 558-3660
http://wvde.state.wv.us

Wisconsin

Higher Educational Aids Board
P.O. Box 7885
Madison, WI 53707-7885
(608) 267-2206
http://heab.state.wi.us
or
Wisconsin Department of Public Instruction
125 South Webster Street
P.O. Box 7841
Madison, WI 53707-7814
(608) 266-3390 or (800) 441-4563
www.dpi.state.wi.us

Wyoming

Wyoming State Department of Education
Hathaway Building
2300 Capitol Avenue, 2nd Floor
Cheyenne, WY 82002-0050
(307) 777-6265
www.k12.wy.us
or
Wyoming Community College Commission
2020 Carey Avenue, 8th Floor
Cheyenne, WY 82002
(307) 777-7763
www.commission.wcc.edu

INDEX

INDEX

ABOUT THE AUTHOR

SUZE ORMAN has been called "a force in the world of personal finance" and a "one-woman financial advice powerhouse" by *USA Today*. A two-time Emmy® Award–winning television show host, *New York Times* best-selling author, magazine and online columnist, writer-producer, and motivational speaker, Suze is undeniably America's most recognized personal finance expert.

Suze has written five consecutive *New York Times* best sellers—*The Money Book for the Young, Fabulous & Broke*; *The Laws of Money, The Lessons of Life*; *The Road to Wealth*; *The Courage to Be Rich*; and *The 9 Steps to Financial Freedom*—as well as the national best sellers *Suze Orman's Financial Guidebook* and *You've Earned It, Don't Lose It*. Her most recent book, *Women & Money*, was published by Spiegel & Grau in February 2007. A newspaper column, also called "Women & Money," syndicated by Universal Press Syndicate, began in January 2007. Additionally, she has created *Suze Orman's*

FICO Kit, Suze Orman's Will & Trust Kit, Suze Orman's Insurance Kit, The Ask Suze Library System, and *Suze Orman's Ultimate Protection Portfolio*.

Suze has written, coproduced, and hosted five PBS specials based on her *New York Times* best-selling books. She is the single most successful fund-raiser in the history of public television, and recently won her second Daytime Emmy® Award in the category of Outstanding Service Show Host. Suze won her first Emmy® in 2004, in the same category.

Suze is contributing editor to *O, The Oprah Magazine* and *O at Home* and has a biweekly column, "Money Matters," on Yahoo! Finance. She hosts her own award-winning national CNBC-TV show, *The Suze Orman Show*, which airs every Saturday night, as well as *Financial Freedom Hour* on QVC television.

Suze has been honored with three American Women in Radio and Television (AWRT) Gracie Allen Awards. This award recognizes the nation's best radio, television, and cable programming for, by, and about women. In 2003, Suze garnered her first Gracie for *The Suze Orman Show* in the National/Network/Sydication Talk Show category. She won her second and third Gracies in the Individual Achievement: Program Host category in 2005 and 2006.

Profiled in *Worth* magazine's 100th issue as among those "who have revolutionized the way America thinks about money," Suze also was named one of *Smart Money* magazine's top thirty "Power Brokers," defined as those who have most influenced the mutual fund industry and affected our money, in 1999. A 2003 inductee into the Books for a Better Life (BBL) Award Hall of Fame in recognition of her ongoing contributions to self-improvement, Suze previously received the 1999 BBL Motivational Book Award for *The Courage to Be Rich*. As a tribute to her continuing involvement, in 2002 the organization established the Suze Orman First Book Award to honor a first-time author of a self-improvement book in any category. She received a 2003 Crossing Borders Award from the Feminist Press. The award recognizes a distinguished group of women who not only have excelled in remarkable careers but also have shown great courage, vision, and conviction by forging new places for women in their respective fields. In 2002, Suze was selected as one of five distinguished recipients of the prestigious TJFR Group News Luminaries Award, which honors lifetime achievement in business journalism.

A sought-after motivational speaker, Suze has lectured widely throughout the United States, South Africa, and Asia to audiences of up to fifty thousand people, often appearing alongside individuals such as Colin Powell, Rudy Giuliani, Jerry Lewis, Steve Forbes, and Donald Trump. She has been featured in almost every major publication in the United States and has appeared numerous times on *The View*, *Larry King Live*, and *The Oprah Winfrey Show*.

A Certified Financial Planner®, Suze directed the Suze Orman Financial Group from 1987 to 1997, served as vice president of investments for Prudential Bache Securities from 1983 to 1987, and from 1980 to 1983 was an account executive at Merrill Lynch. Prior to that, she worked as a waitress at the Buttercup Bakery in Berkeley, California, from 1973 to 1980.